ANNIE MAHLE

HOME AT SEA

RECIPES FROM A MAINE WINDJAMMER

SECOND EDITION
THE RED BOOK

At Home At Sea: Recipes from a Maine Windjammer
2nd Edition

Original book design by MORE & Co.
Supporting design by Kara Plikaitis
Copyediting by Norma Mahle, Jesse Ellis, Elizabeth Poisson

Printed in the United States of America by Kirkwood Printing, Wilmington, MA
Printed locally, on recycled paper, because we believe in sustainable interactions
with our neighbors and our earth.

ISBN: 978-0-9749706-3-9
Library of Congress Control Number: 2017943697

Baggywrinkle Publishing
136 Holmes Street
Rockland, Maine 04841
1-800-869-0604
www.athomeatsea.com
www.mainewindjammer.com

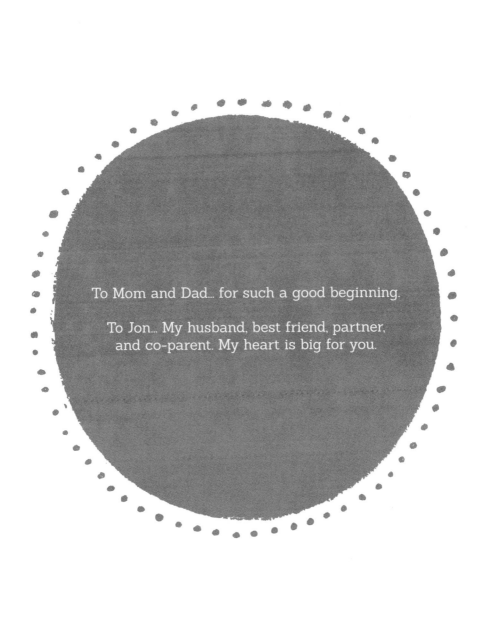

To Mom and Dad... for such a good beginning.

To Jon... My husband, best friend, partner,
and co-parent. My heart is big for you.

Contents

Introduction

I believe in food cooked with the freshest ingredients: using my hands to shape bread; taking time and care when I'm cooking; and sitting at the table with friends and family to share the soul-filled food we've created. I love the smell, shape, feel, and look of pure ingredients. I hope that our daughters have learned by example that the most precious and sacred time of the day is dinnertime, when we come together at the close of our days with loved ones to share, discuss, argue, and agree. To me, this is true nourishment. While "fast food" may be convenient, fully nourishing ourselves is more than simply removing the empty feeling in our bellies. Food is a way that we can connect - to our families and to nature.

This wasn't always the way I thought about food and cooking. I came to it by a roundabout way— falling in love with sailing, Maine, and my husband and co-owner of the *Riggin*, Captain Jon Finger.

How It Started, or "Not the Navy Blue Suit, Thank You"

Before I came to Maine, working in restaurants was a way for me to earn money, not a passion. My first jobs were in the kitchens of restaurants, but they weren't places where the craft and the passion of good food was evident— anywhere. I couldn't say that I was satisfied with the ingredients going into what I was making or, obviously, the final product. Most of it was food made on a large scale for huge numbers of people and presented in a way that did nothing to enhance the dining experience.

Working my way through college in kitchens I wasn't proud of, I arrived at my senior year at Michigan State University about to graduate with a B.S. in Psychology. Everyone kept telling me that I couldn't "do anything" with only an undergraduate degree in Psychology and my glib response was always that I would get an advanced degree. But, by the time I was into my senior year of college, I knew that I could not stomach one more second of school, much less the four more years required to get a Ph.D.

So, I had the brilliant idea to "take a year off". I decided I wanted to travel, I wanted to learn how to sail, and I needed to make enough money so that I wouldn't have to call home. Why travel? Save a brief summer in Europe, I'd only lived in the Midwest— I wanted to experience something different. Why sailing? Again, it was different, outside, physical, and… different.

A few weeks before I graduated from college, needing a job, I met the daughter of the owners of the Schooner *Stephen Taber*, a Maine windjammer. With the realization that I could actually get paid to sail, I called about a job in the Maine windjammer fleet. I talked with Ellen Barnes, then co-owner and Cook on the *Taber*. She said if I could be in Rockland, Maine the day after I graduated, I had a job as a mess cook. Wahoo! I was so excited I got off the phone before asking how much the job paid, or even what a mess cook was. Ellen's daughter and I got up at 4 a.m. (I was much more accustomed to getting to sleep around 4 a.m.) and drove 16 hours from Michigan to Maine. I got up again at the same unearthly hour the next day and started my first day as Mess Cook.

I found out quickly that a mess cook is aptly named. I cleaned up after the mess maker, the cook, all summer long. Amid all of the chopping and cleaning, I learned about baking from scratch, slow-cooked food, and woodstoves. This was my first

exposure to the real craft of creating soulful food— food made with pride, good ingredients, time, thoughtfulness, and care.

My plan that year was to sail for one summer, then get a "real job", something 9 to 5 where I'd be wearing a navy blue suit, and start working toward a Ph.D. .... The next year, my plan was to sail for two summers and then get a "real job", something 9 to 5 where I'd be wearing a navy blue suit. Never happened. I'd fallen in love with sailing, Maine, and Jon Finger.

Jon was also from the Midwest; he grew up right next to Lake Michigan and spent his summers sailing. He paid one dollar for his first boat, which was missing sails, a rudder, and other unimportant items— all of which he fabricated. When he was sixteen, he had his first sail on a windjammer. From then on, he knew he wanted to be a captain of one of these majestic vessels. After four years in the Coast Guard, two of those on the U.S. Barque *Eagle* (our ambassador ship for the United States), he came to the Maine windjammer fleet. He spent the next ten years working for other captains in the fleet, in Bermuda on a research vessel, and running his own daysailer.

My first glimpse of Jon was my first morning in the galley, as he peered at me over the watermelon that he was balancing precariously on top of an armload of boxed groceries. It wasn't the last I'd see of him. Whenever I had a break, I'd sneak back to the quarterdeck and get him to teach me something about sailing. While later I'd become passionate about cooking, when I was a mess cook it was a means to an end. I really wanted to learn how to sail and so I spent every available second on deck. We are a perfect example of opposites attracting. I am loud, lively, busy, talkative, and laugh a lot. Jon is calm, steady, thoughtful, quiet, and kind— a perfect captain. While we tried to keep our interest in each other a secret, it's hard to do in such a small community! It was obvious to both of us early on that we wanted to build a life with each other and grow older together.

The following summer I became a deckhand on the *Taber* while Jon moved on to run his own friendship sloop *Grace O'Malley* as a daysailer. After spending that one summer apart, we realized that we liked being together far more than we did being separated. We also realized that while we wanted to work on the same ship, we needed to have separate areas of responsibility. So, I chose to move back into the galley. By this time, I had discovered that this really was no sacrifice as I could come up on deck and do all of the fun deck stuff, like driving the yawl boat, hauling on sails and tacking, but if the weather became cold and rainy, all of a sudden, I would need to "check my pies" in the galley by the warm, dry stove.

The Craft of Cooking

After three summers in the fleet— one year as a mess cook, one as deckhand, and one as head cook on the *Victory Chimes*— I decided I wanted to learn more about the craft and the art of cooking. While I'd been cooking for several years, I knew there was a lot more I didn't know, like how to correct a dish if something untoward happened. What if I forgot about the bread rising since early morning and it looked like Jabba the Hut? I needed to learn the why of cooking and I found that at Jessica's European Bistro.

Jessica's was the best restaurant in the area at the time and our favorite. After two interviews, numerous phone calls, and an offer to work for free, the owner, Hans Bucher, hired me as Sous Chef and quickly became my mentor. The time spent under Hans' tutelage taught me traditional European-style cooking. I learned about the delight of making food taste and look good all the time. Hans is a Swiss-trained chef and the youngest executive chef at the Hyatt when he first came to the U.S. He is of Swiss-German descent and I of German descent, so sometimes we butted heads! Hans like to listen to country music. All. Day. Long. After a time, I became not only tolerant, but a fan. So much so that when I first left Jessica's, I couldn't cook without country music playing in the background.

It was during this time that Jon and I married. Bagpipes skirling, we were piped into an outdoor chapel and married by Captains Ken and Ellen Barnes— the people who had first introduced us. After the ceremony, we had a champagne toast on the *Victory Chimes* and a reception catered by Hans at our house.

I spent three years under Hans' mentorship. After a time, adventure beckoned and Jon and I headed south. We were hired as Captain and Chef for a yacht owned by a retired New York Trust banker, spending the summers in New England and the winters in the Caribbean. It was our job to take out either the owner or charter guests for week-long trips.

Working on a private yacht is about as far away from Maine windjamming as a person can get and still be sailing. Cooking for a maximum of four guests, offers wonderful opportunities to be creative, to plate all of our meals individually, and to indulge our guests' whims. I also learned to fold towels so neatly and uniformly that Martha Stewart would have been put to shame. It's a very precise life.

What I loved most about the tropical islands of the Caribbean was shopping in the local markets for fruits, vegetables, and spices. The local women peddling their produce were always a highlight of my week. I also enjoyed the challenge of planning menus around the dietary needs and preferences of our passengers, I liked it best if I could meet the folks when they boarded and then decide what I would cook for them. It was a real treat to be able to tailor the meals to suit the small group on board.

This is where I developed a Caribbean influence in my cooking, using more fruits and salsas.

Every summer Jon and I would bring the yacht up to Maine to charter during the month of August. We would invariably arrive at night, but we always knew when we'd arrived home - the scent of pine trees greeted us. We would stand on deck with our heads thrown back looking up at the canopy of stars and taking in big gulps of the fragrance of pine.

Sometimes the yachting world seems more romantic than it really is. After dusting electrical panels with dental picks, cleaning toilets with toothbrushes, and polishing oily engine blocks until they sparkled like mirrors, we longed for the simplicity of Maine. Three years in the lucrative yachting business allowed us the freedom to return home to Maine, where our hearts live, and buy or start a business. Jon tells the story of driving all the way from Indiana to Maine for the first time. When he stepped out of the car and breathed in, he knew he'd found the place where his heart was most full. I feel the same. I feel less encumbered in Maine than I do anywhere else I've ever traveled or lived.

We briefly considered and discarded opening a restaurant, a bed and breakfast, or a bakery. While all were interesting, only a Maine windjammer allowed us to work together and more importantly raise our family together, as by this time I was pregnant with our first child, Chlöe.

Would you like some schooner with your coffee?

On a crisp September Saturday in 1997, Jon found Dave Allen, the then owner of the *J. & E. Riggin*, changing the oil in the schooner's 20-year-old yawl boat. Yawl boats are beautiful wooden workboats for vessels without inboard engines (as is the case with many boats in the fleet). They serve as a tugboat for moving the vessels in and out of tight harbors, and as a shuttle to get folks ashore. Dave was grunting (and swearing) with bloody knuckles and oil running down his arm from wrist to elbow as he held the greasy oil filter up for inspection. Dave, only half joking, asked Jon if he wanted to buy a schooner. Jon, not joking at all, said yes. Off to breakfast we went to agree on a price. Two months later the *J. & E. Riggin* was ours.

Some might argue that you never buy something without test-driving it first and, again we would agree. Nevertheless, our first sail on the *Riggin* was the day we left the dock with our first group of passengers. This is not quite as strange as it seems. By the time we bought the *Riggin*, we knew all the boats in the fleet and how they sailed. Still it was a bit of a surprise to a guest on our first trip out when he asked Jon how long we'd been sailing the *Riggin*. Jon looked at his watch and said, with his usual straight-guy face, "Oh, about two hours." Jon was so comfortable at the wheel the guest assumed he'd been doing it for years!

We've "owned" the *J. & E. Riggin* since 1998. Jon and I don't really view it as ownership, but rather stewardship. This is our tenure. We will eventually pass this National Historic Landmark, a beautiful example of our collective American history, on to another. It will be their turn to have this fantastic life, sharing the Coast of Maine with guests in this time-honored way.

Annie
May 2017
Lat 44N 5'47.93" Long 69W 7'1.47"
Rockland, Maine

Breakfast

The rich aromas of wood smoke and our own special blend of coffee greet our guests as they rise to take their first cup of coffee, tea, or cocoa on deck. The smell of sizzling bacon, or granola roasting in the oven, follows. As more guests rise for the day, the sounds of soft laughter and camaraderie mix with the sounds of nature. The air is crisp and bright or maybe misty with a morning fog that has yet to burn off.

RECIPES

French Toast

I will use almost any leftover bread for this recipe. This is a good example of leftovers being better the second time around. Serves 4

4 large eggs
2 cups whole milk
4 teaspoons sugar
$1/2$ teaspoon ground cinnamon
1 teaspoon vanilla extract
1 teaspoon rum— if it's for grown-ups
salted butter for the skillet
12 slices day-old Crusty Peasant or French bread

Whisk all of the ingredients except the butter and bread in a medium bowl. Heat a griddle or skillet over medium heat and rub with butter. While the pan is heating, soak the bread slices in the batter (be sure both sides are coated) and immediately place the slices on the heated skillet. Cook until golden brown on the bottom, flip the bread, and continue to cook until the other side is brown. Set the toast aside on a plate in a warm oven while the rest is still cooking.

Variations
I often make a special French Toast with cream cheese and jam in the center of two slices of bread. Here are my favorite combinations

Cranberry Orange: **Cranberry Orange Bread** (page 162), marmalade, and cream cheese
Pumpkin Cream: **Pumpkin Bread** (page 163) and cream cheese
Raspberry Cream: French bread, raspberry jam, and cream cheese

Aunt Rita's Double Toffee Coffee Cake

This recipe is one that graced most of our holiday brunches when I was growing up. The pudding mixes serve to make this a super moist cake that still has some structure to it. The caramel and butterscotch flavors? Well, let's just say it's a wonderful food memory from my childhood. Serves 12

Streusel
1½ cups firmly packed light brown sugar
1 cup chopped walnuts
1 tablespoon ground cinnamon

Cake
2 cups all-purpose flour
1 (3.5-ounce) package instant vanilla pudding mix
1 (3.5-ounce) package instant butterscotch pudding mix
1 cup sugar
2 teaspoons baking powder
1 teaspoon table salt
1 cup water
¾ cup canola oil
1 teaspoon vanilla extract
4 large eggs

Streusel
Blend the streusel ingredients with a pastry knife in a small bowl and set aside.

Cake
Preheat oven to 350°F. Lightly grease a 9- x 13-inch pan. Sift the flour, both pudding mixes, sugar, baking powder, and salt into a large bowl. Make a well in the center of the flour mixture and add the rest of the cake ingredients. Whisk from the center out to the edges of the bowl until just combined. Transfer half the batter to the prepared baking pan and sprinkle with half the streusel. Repeat. Bake for 40 to 45 minutes or until a toothpick inserted into the center comes out clean and the center springs back when lightly pressed. Cool in the pan on a wire rack.

Annie's Famous Granola

I often add dried fruit (raisins, pineapple, or cranberries) to the granola. If you do add dried fruit, don't bake it, but stir it into the granola just after you've taken the granola out of the oven. Makes 12 cups

$^1\!/_2$ cup honey
$^3\!/_4$ cup canola oil
2 teaspoons vanilla extract
4 cups old-fashioned rolled oats
2 cups bran buds
$1^1\!/_2$ cups unsweetened coconut flakes
$1^1\!/_2$ cups chopped walnuts

Preheat oven to 250°F. Heat the honey, oil, and vanilla in a small pot over medium-low heat until the honey is warm and loose. Meanwhile, combine the remaining ingredients together in a large bowl. Pour the honey mixture over the dry ingredients and combine thoroughly. Spread the granola evenly onto a large baking pan (you may need two pans, depending on their size). Bake for 1 hour or until the mixture is golden brown, stirring often. Add any dried fruit once the granola is removed from the oven. Cool completely and store in an airtight container. Serve with oatmeal and/or yogurt.

Fruit Compote

This compote is great on top of oatmeal, which is how we serve it on the boat. In the winter, my daughters, Ella and Chlöe, like it warmed up for breakfast with a little yogurt or milk in it. Below is my favorite combination of fruits, but I've also used currants, dried cranberries and dried blueberries. For special occasions, use a little rum or Grand Marnier in place of $^1\!/_4$ cup of the apple juice. And it tastes even better the next day! Makes 4 cups

1 cup dried apricots, coarsely chopped
1 cup raisins
1 cup prunes, coarsely chopped
1 fresh apple, cored, peeled, and diced
$^1\!/_4$ cup firmly packed light brown sugar
$^3\!/_4$ teaspoon ground cinnamon
2 cups apple juice

Add all ingredients to a medium saucepan and bring to a boil over medium-high heat. Reduce heat to low, cover, and simmer for 30 to 40 minutes or until the fruit is soft and all cooked together. Serve warm or cold.

Buttermilk Pancakes

Makes 10 pancakes

1½ cups all-purpose flour
2 tablespoons sugar
1 teaspoon baking powder
¼ teaspoon baking soda
½ teaspoon table salt
1⅓ cups buttermilk
1 large egg
¼ cup (½ stick) salted butter, melted and cooled (plus more for the griddle)

Place a sifter into the bottom of a large bowl. Measure the flour, sugar, baking powder, baking soda, and salt into the sifter and sift into the bowl. Make a well in the flour mixture and add the buttermilk, egg, and butter, stirring from the center of the well out to the edges of the bowl. If you'd like, gently fold in any of the fruits or nuts in the variations listed (see below). Do not overmix.

Heat a griddle or skillet over medium heat until hot and then lightly coat with butter. Ladle the batter onto the griddle. When the pancakes start to set and you see bubbles popping on the pancakes, flip them and cook until the other side is brown. Keep the cooked pancakes in a warm oven until all the pancakes are done.

Variations
Blueberry Pancakes: Add 1½ cups fresh Maine blueberries.
Apple Walnut Pancakes: Add 1½ total cups chopped apples and walnuts (combined).
Banana Pancakes: Add 1½ cups sliced bananas.
Pumpkin Oatmeal Pancakes: Reduce by ½ cup flour and add ½ cup cooked oatmeal and 1 cup pumpkin puree.

Crêpes Eggs Benedict

This is a meal we have only once a year in our household and that's Christmas morning. My mom started this tradition when I was a child and Jon and I carry it forward with our family in Maine. When the girls were small, it seemed like an endless meal to prepare, but now that they are full participants, each person receives a job and the whole affair goes fairly quickly. There are so many eggs in this recipe that the cholesterol police will be unhappy, but it's so good, it's worth it. Serves 4

Crêpes
1¼ cups all-purpose flour
4 large eggs
1 cup whole milk
1¼ cups cold water
3 tablespoons unsalted butter, melted (plus extra for the skillet)
½ teaspoon table salt

Hollandaise
4 egg yolks
¼ teaspoon table salt
½ teaspoon dry mustard
1 tablespoon fresh lemon juice; about ½ lemon
½ cup (1 stick) unsalted butter

8 large eggs
8 slices Canadian bacon

Overall Instructions
Make the crêpe batter first (page 21). While it's resting, make the Hollandaise (page 21). Warm the serving plates in the oven. Once the crêpe batter is done resting, have one family member cook the crêpes. When the crêpes are nearly done, have another family member cook the Canadian bacon over medium-high heat (you are really just heating it up, so no need to go crazy here) and poach the eggs. Gather an assembly line to put the crêpes together. Place a crêpe on one of the warmed plates. Place the bacon in the center of the crêpe, then the poached egg on the bacon. Fold both sides of the crêpe over then gently roll the crêpe over so the edges of the crêpe are on the bottom. Repeat until all the eggs are gone then ladle the Hollandaise sauce over the crêpes and serve immediately.

Crêpes

Pulse the crêpe ingredients at high speed in a blender or food processor for 30 seconds. Scrape down the sides and blend at least 30 seconds longer. Refrigerate for at least 30 minutes to rest the batter. Heat a small nonstick sauté pan over medium heat for 3 minutes. When it's hot, melt 1 teaspoon of butter and ladle ¼ cup crepe batter into the pan. Tilt the pan to coat the bottom and when you can see bubbles have formed, flip it. Place the finished crêpes on a plate in a warm oven (Don't worry if the first crêpe is a loss — it usually is — the next ones will be fine. You shouldn't need butter after the first crêpe).

Hollandaise

This is my mom's recipe for Hollandaise and it works. Mom's Hollandaise is a bit more foolproof than the traditional method — easier on the arms, as well. You can also use a whisk to combine all the ingredients — the Hollandaise ends up fluffier but it's a bit trickier to do. Put the egg yolks, salt, mustard and lemon juice in blender. Cover and blend. Heat the butter until it is hot. Pour the butter into the running blender in a steady stream. Keep the Hollandaise warm over a hot water bath until you are ready to serve.

Toasted Oatmeal

Serves 4

1 tablespoon unsalted butter
1 cup steel cut oats (or old-fashioned rolled oats)
3 cups water
1 cup whole milk
¼ teaspoon table salt
1 teaspoon ground cinnamon
¼ cup firmly packed light brown sugar

Heat the butter in a large saucepan over medium heat until it just begins to foam. Add the oats, stirring frequently with a wooden spoon, until golden and fragrant, about 1½ to 2 minutes. Add the rest of the ingredients and bring to a simmer. Cook uncovered, stirring occasionally, until the mixture thickens, about 40 minutes (20 minutes for old-fashioned oats). Remove from heat and let the oatmeal stand, uncovered, for 5 minutes before serving.

Serve with Greek yogurt, fruit compote, dried fruit, nuts, fresh berries, maple syrup, honey . . . The list is long and the combinations endless.

Apricot Coffee Cake

Serves 12

Streusel
1/4 cup (1/2 stick) unsalted butter
1/2 cup firmly packed light brown sugar
1/2 cup all-purpose flour
pinch table salt
1/2 cup chopped dried apricots

Cake
1/2 cup (1 stick) unsalted butter, room temperature
    (plus more for baking pan)
1 1/2 cups firmly packed light brown sugar
4 large eggs
1 cup whole milk
3 cups all-purpose flour
4 teaspoons baking powder
1 teaspoon table salt

Streusel
Blend the streusel ingredients except the apricots with a pastry knife in a small bowl.
Add the apricots and set aside.

Cake
Preheat oven to 350°F. Lightly grease a 9- x 13-inch baking pan. Cream the butter
and sugar in a large bowl with a wooden spoon or the bowl of a stand mixer with the
paddle attachment. Add the eggs and then the milk. Place a sifter on top of a small
plate and measure dry ingredients into the sifter. Sift over the batter and mix until just
blended. Transfer half the batter to the prepared baking pan and sprinkle with half
the streusel. Repeat. Bake for 30 minutes or until a toothpick inserted into the center
comes out clean and the center springs back when lightly pressed. Cool in the pan on
a wire rack.

Three-Grain Pancakes

Makes 12 pancakes

$^3/_4$ cup all-purpose flour
$^1/_2$ cup whole wheat flour
$^1/_2$ cup rye flour
$^1/_4$ cup cornmeal
$1^1/_2$ tablespoons sugar
1 tablespoon baking powder
1 teaspoon table salt
$^1/_4$ teaspoon baking soda
$1^1/_2$ cups whole milk
3 large eggs
3 tablespoons unsalted butter, melted (plus extra for the griddle)

Sift the dry ingredients into a large bowl. Make a well in the flour mixture. Stir in the milk, and eggs, and melted butter until just combined. Do not overmix. Let the mixture stand for 20 to 30 minutes, this will soften and hydrate the flours and cornmeal.

Heat a griddle or skillet over medium heat until hot and then lightly coat with butter. Ladle the batter onto the griddle. When the pancakes start to set and you see bubbles popping on the pancakes, flip them and cook until the other side is brown. Keep the cooked pancakes in a warm oven until all the pancakes are done.

Mocha Syrup Makes 3 cups

$2^1/_2$ cups coffee

1 cup firmly packed light brown
  sugar

$^1/_2$ cup cocoa powder

pinch table salt

1 teaspoon ground cinnamon

1 tablespoon vanilla extract

1 cup coarsely chopped
  walnuts (optional)

Combine all ingredients except vanilla in a medium sauce pan and bring to a boil over medium high heat whisking occasionally. Boil for 10 minutes or until mixture thickens to coat the back of a spoon. Remove from heat, add the vanilla and serve warm with pancakes or over ice cream. Garnish with walnuts.

German Apple Pancake

Serves 4

$^1/_2$ cup unbleached all-purpose flour
1 tablespoon sugar
$^1/_2$ teaspoon table salt
$^2/_3$ cup half and half
2 large eggs
1 teaspoon vanilla extract
2 tablespoons unsalted butter
$1^1/_4$ pounds Granny Smith or Braeburn apples, peeled, quartered,
    and cored; about 5 small apples
$^1/_4$ cup firmly packed light brown sugar
$^1/_4$ teaspoon ground cinnamon
1 teaspoon fresh lemon juice
confectioner's sugar for dusting

Preheat oven to 500°F. Adjust your oven rack to a middle/upper position. Whisk the flour, white sugar, and salt together in medium bowl. Measure the half and half in a liquid measuring cup and add the eggs and vanilla. Whisk the wet and dry ingredients together until no lumps remain, about 20 seconds. Set the batter aside.

Heat the butter in a 10-inch oven-proof skillet over medium-high heat until sizzling. Add the apples and stir frequently for about 10 minutes or until the apples are golden brown. Add the brown sugar, cinnamon, and lemon juice and stir until the sugar has dissolved.

Working quickly, pour the batter into the skillet around and over the apples. Place the skillet in the oven and immediately reduce heat to 425°F. Bake for 10 to 15 minutes or until the pancake edges are brown and puffy, and have risen above edges of skillet.

Loosen the edges of the pancake with a heatproof rubber spatula. Transfer the pancake onto a serving platter, dust with confectioner's sugar, cut into wedges, and serve.

Frittata

This recipe is so versatile and, more often than not, we have it for dinner on a weeknight during the winter with a salad of mixed greens. On the boat, we have it more commonly for breakfast or lunch and routinely substitute seasonal fresh garden vegetables for what's listed here. Serves 4 to 6

2 tablespoons extra virgin olive oil
2 cups thinly sliced zucchini; about 2 medium zucchini

6 ounces button mushrooms, sliced; about 2 cups
1 cup thinly sliced red bell pepper; about ½ pepper
1 teaspoon kosher salt
several grinds fresh black pepper
½ teaspoon Dijon mustard
8 large eggs
2 ounces grated Parmesan cheese; about 1 cup lightly packed

Preheat oven to 350°F. Heat a 10-inch cast-iron skillet over medium-high heat and add the olive oil. Add the veggies, salt, and pepper and sauté for 7 to 10 minutes or until just tender. Whisk the mustard, eggs, and ½ cup Parmesan cheese in a medium bowl and pour the mixture over the veggies. Transfer the skillet to the oven and bake for 30 to 35 minutes or until the frittata has puffed up and is only ever so slightly jiggly in the center. Remove from oven and sprinkle with the remaining ½ cup of cheese and serve immediately.

Variations
The sky is really the limit here and I often use small bits of leftovers in this frittata to clear out the fridge. Some of my favorite substitutions are asparagus, kale, tomatoes, or potatoes for the veggies and cheddar, Gouda, Havarti, or Fontina for the cheese.

Sue's Breakfast Muffins

Sue is my mom's best friend and when our families would get together at her camp over the summer, she would make these for breakfast. There were a lot of hungry mouths to feed with four families and a total of 16 kids. The moms would bake for what seemed like hours and as soon as these muffins were out of the oven and coated with butter and sugar, they would disappear with only sticky fingers left to lick clean. On the boat, we now affectionately call these muffins "Sugar Bombs." Makes 12 muffins

Muffins
²/₃ cup unsalted butter, room temperature
1 cup sugar
2 large eggs
1 cup whole milk
3 cups all-purpose flour
1 tablespoon baking powder
1 teaspoon table salt
¹/₄ teaspoon ground nutmeg

Topping
1 cup sugar
2 teaspoons ground cinnamon
³/₄ cup (1¹/₂ sticks) salted butter, melted

Muffins
Preheat oven to 350°F. Lightly grease a 12-cup muffin pan. Cream the butter and sugar in a medium-sized bowl with a wooden spoon or the bowl of a stand mixer with the paddle attachment. Add the egg and milk and mix well. Sift in the dry ingredients and mix until just combined. Fill the prepared muffin cups two-thirds full. Bake for 20 to 25 minutes or until a toothpick comes out clean and the muffins spring back when lightly pressed.

Topping
Combine the sugar and cinnamon in a small bowl. When the muffins are done, dip each muffin in the melted butter and immediately roll it in the cinnamon-sugar mixture.

Shirred Eggs

Serves 2

1 teaspoon extra virgin olive oil (plus extra for the ramekins)
2 cups baby spinach lightly packed
pinch table salt (for both the spinach and the eggs)
$^1/_4$ cup diced prosciutto
2 slices tomato
1 ounce grated cheddar cheese; about $^1/_4$ cup lightly packed
4 large eggs
$^1/_4$ cup heavy cream
several grinds fresh black pepper

Preheat oven to 375°F. Rub the inside of 2, 8-ounce ramekins with oil. Heat a medium-sized skillet over high heat. Add the oil, spinach, and salt and cook for 1 minute or until the spinach has just wilted. Divide the spinach evenly between the 2 ramekins. Evenly divide and layer the prosciutto, tomato slices, cheese, eggs, and the heavy cream. Bake for 18 to 23 minutes or until the whites of the eggs are just done. Serve immediately.

Sour Cream Coffee Cake

The base of this recipe comes from A Taste of the Taber *cookbook, I've added a number of riffs and variations over the years to this classic coffee cake which often shows up for breakfast one morning during a trip.* Serves 9

Streusel
1/2 cup chopped walnuts
1/2 cup sugar
2 teaspoons ground cinnamon

Cake
3/4 cup (1 1/2 sticks) unsalted butter, room temperature
3/4 cup sugar
2 cups all-purpose flour
1/2 teaspoon table salt
1 teaspoon baking powder
1 teaspoon baking soda
1/2 cup plain yogurt
1/2 cup sour cream
2 large eggs
1 teaspoon vanilla extract

Streusel
Combine the streusel ingredients in a small bowl and set aside.

Cake
Preheat oven to 350°F. Lightly grease a 9- x 9-inch baking pan. Cream the butter and sugar in a large bowl with a wooden spoon or the bowl of a stand mixer with the paddle attachment. Sift in the flour, salt, baking powder, and baking soda and combine. Add the yogurt, sour cream, eggs, and vanilla and stir until just combined. Spoon the batter into the prepared pan and sprinkle with the streusel. Bake for 40 to 45 minutes or until a toothpick inserted into the center comes out clean and the center springs back when lightly pressed. Cool in the pan on a wire rack.

Variations
Blueberry Maple: Replace the Streusel with 1/3 cup maple sugar. Replace the vanilla extract with maple extract. Add 1 1/2 cups fresh or frozen blueberries to the batter. If using frozen blueberries, add another 15 minutes to the baking time.
Espresso Cinnamon: Add 1 teaspoon espresso powder to the Streusel. Add another 1 teaspoon to the dry ingredients of the batter.

Dressings & Condiments

While I love big, bold flavors, when it comes to salads, simple is sometimes best. Freshly harvested greens drizzled with a squeeze of lemon juice and a dab of extra virgin olive oil; sprinkled with a pinch of sea salt and fresh black pepper can be the most special of salads when the ingredients are just right. Simple preparation allows each ingredient its own voice and character.

Creamy Blue Cheese Dressing

Makes 1 cup

2$\frac{1}{2}$ ounces crumbled blue cheese; about $\frac{1}{2}$ cup
5 tablespoons buttermilk
3 tablespoons sour cream
2 tablespoons mayonnaise
2 teaspoons white wine vinegar
$\frac{1}{4}$ teaspoon sugar
1 teaspoon minced garlic; about 1 clove
$\frac{1}{8}$ teaspoon kosher salt
several grinds fresh black pepper
dash of Worcestershire sauce

Combine all the ingredients together in a small bowl. Refrigerate for up to 2 weeks.

Creamy Herb Dressing

Makes about 2 cups

2 tablespoons fresh minced dill
2 tablespoons fresh minced Italian parsley
2 tablespoons fresh minced thyme
2 tablespoons fresh minced chives
$\frac{3}{4}$ cup mayonnaise
$\frac{1}{2}$ cup buttermilk
2 tablespoons apple cider vinegar
$\frac{1}{2}$ teaspoon kosher salt
several grinds fresh black pepper
$\frac{3}{4}$ teaspoon Tabasco or other hot sauce

Pulse all the ingredients in a blender. Refrigerate for up to 2 weeks.

Lime Ginger Dressing

Makes 1 cup

1 teaspoon minced garlic; about 1 clove
1 teaspoon grated fresh ginger
1 teaspoon Dijon mustard
$\frac{1}{3}$ cup fresh lime juice; about 3 limes
1 tablespoon soy sauce
$\frac{2}{3}$ cup canola oil

Combine all ingredients but the canola oil in a blender and then slowly add the oil.

Red Pepper Jam

Makes 2 cups

4 large red bell peppers, cored, seeded, and coarsely chopped
1 tablespoon kosher salt
$^1/_4$ teaspoon red pepper flakes
$1^1/_2$ cups apple cider vinegar
$2^1/_2$ cups sugar

Place the peppers in a food processor and pulse until minced. Sprinkle with the salt and let them sit for 30 minutes. Rinse the peppers in cold water and drain the excess water. Transfer the peppers into a wide, heavy saucepan and add the red pepper flakes, vinegar, and sugar. Bring the mixture to a boil and stir occasionally for 15 to 20 minutes or until a candy thermometer reads 220°F. Ladle the jam into hot, sterilized jars and seal. Alternately, store in the refrigerator for up to two weeks.

Lemon Aioli

Makes 1 cup

1 small clove garlic, smashed and coarsely chopped
1 egg yolk
1 teaspoon Dijon mustard
1 teaspoon lemon zest, zest from about one lemon
2 teaspoons lemon juice
dash Worcestershire
$1/8$ teaspoon salt
several grinds of fresh black pepper
2 tablespoons extra virgin olive oil
$1/2$ cup canola oil

Combine all ingredients except oil in a food processor and pulse until combined. Ever so slowly, while the motor is running, add the oil. After about a minute of dribbling the oil in, you can add it more quickly.

Pickled Shallots

Makes 2 cups

$3/4$ cup plus 2 tablespoons rice wine vinegar
2 tablespoons apple cider vinegar
$1/4$ cup water
2 tablespoons sugar
1 tablespoon kosher salt
2 cups finely sliced shallots

Bring the vinegars, water, sugar, and salt to a boil in a medium-sized sauce pan. Add the onions and combine. Transfer to a pint-sized ball jar and refrigerate for up to 2 weeks.

Appetizers

After an exhilarating day of sailing, our faces smiling and wind-burned, the crew and guests furl the huge canvas sails, clear the deck, and enjoy a time of rest. The backdrop to this time of day may be granite rocks covered in seaweed, a curious seal popping up to see what's what, or soaring ospreys searching for their dinners as the sun sinks on the horizon.

Artichoke and Red Pepper Dip

This can be made ahead of time and stored in the fridge or freezer until you're ready to bake it..
Makes 3 cups

1 (8-ounce) jar marinated artichokes, liquid drained
1 (7-ounce) can green chilies
1 (7-ounce) jar roasted red peppers, liquid drained
½ cup mayonnaise
½ cup salsa, fresh or prepared
8 ounces grated cheddar or Monterey Jack cheese; about 2 cups
    lightly packed
several grinds fresh black pepper

Preheat oven to 400°F. Pulse all of the ingredients in a food processor and then spoon the mixture onto a large oven-proof platter or shallow casserole dish. Bake for 15 to 20 minutes or until bubbly and lightly brown on top. Serve with crackers or corn chips.

Green Olive Tapenade

This tapenade can be made up to two weeks in advance— it only gets better with time. My favorite way to serve it is with goat cheese and homemade crostini or crackers.. Makes 1 cup

1 cup green olives, pitted
2 tablespoons capers
2 anchovy fillets
½ cup lightly packed fresh Italian parsley leaves
2 cloves garlic
¼ cup extra virgin olive oil
several grinds fresh black pepper

Because the olives and capers are so salty, soak them in fresh water for a few minutes to release some of the salt. Transfer to a strainer. Purée all the ingredients in a food processor. Refrigerate until ready to serve. Serve with Crostini (page 39).

Caramelized Onion and Gorgonzola Tart

Serves 4 to 6

1 frozen puff pastry sheet
1 teaspoon unsalted butter
4 cups thinly sliced onions; about 2 large onions
1 tablespoon brandy
4 ounces crumbled Gorgonzola cheese; about 1 cup
several grinds fresh black pepper

Preheat oven to 375°F. Set the puff pastry out to defrost slightly. Meanwhile, melt
the butter in a large sauté pan over medium heat. Add the onions and cook, stirring
frequently for 20 to 30 minutes or until they are a golden-brown color (you may need
to turn the heat down so they don't burn). Add the brandy and cook another minute
or two.

Place the defrosted pastry on an ungreased baking pan and roll the sides over once
or twice to create an edge for the tart. Spread the onions evenly onto the pastry then
sprinkle the Gorgonzola and pepper on top. Bake for 15 minutes or until the crust is
brown and the cheese is melted. Slice and serve as an appetizer or with a large green
salad as a dinner.

Variations
Peperonata: Reduce onions by 2 cups and add red and yellow bell peppers
by 2 cups.
Caramelized Onion and Brie: Replace Gorgonzola with Brie or Fontina.
Kalamata and Tomato: Add black olives and diced tomatoes.
Leftover: Add little bits of cheese, veggies, or meat that are leftover and hanging out in
your fridge.

Crostini are slices of bread drizzled with olive oil and toasted. They're
easy to make and dress up any appetizers. I'll often make an extra loaf
of bread so that I can serve crostini with appetizers. To make crostini,
slice a loaf of French or Italian bread into ¼-inch slices. Place them
on a baking sheet and drizzle with olive oil. Bake at 350°F until golden
brown.

Herbed Feta Cheese

This recipe is especially practical when the herb garden is flush with more herbs than a chef can possibly use. If you don't have an herb garden of your own, perhaps borrowing from a friend or finding a bouquet of herbs at the farmer's market is the way to go. Serves 6 to 8

1 pound piece (or several large chunks) good quality feta cheese
8 to 10 fresh sage leaves
2 to 3 fresh dill sprigs
4 sprigs fresh thyme
4 sprigs fresh Greek oregano
4 sprigs fresh Italian parsley
1 teaspoon whole black peppercorns
$1/2$ teaspoon crushed red pepper
1 lemon, thinly sliced (plus extra for garnish)
extra virgin olive oil as needed
2 to 3 ripe tomatoes, sliced for garnish
sprigs of herbs for garnish

Place the cheese, herbs, spices, and lemon slices in a resealable plastic bag. Add olive oil until the cheese is liberally coated. Press out the air in the bag, seal, and refrigerate at least 6 hours (24 hours is even better).

To serve, remove the cheese from the bag, reserving the oil. Cut the cheese into bite-size slices and arrange the slices on a platter with the sliced lemon and tomatoes. Drizzle with some of the reserved oil and garnish with herbs. Serve at room temperature with crackers or pita bread.

Lobster Dip

The idea of having leftover lobster will seem absurd to most everyone who doesn't live in Maine, I know. However, after our weekly lobster bakes we often find we are able to treat ourselves to lobster a second time. This one is so simple. Serves 4 to 6

1 cup coarsely chopped cooked lobster meat; about 1 (1-pound) lobster
$1/4$ cup Hellmann's mayonnaise
Worcestershire sauce to taste
several grinds fresh black pepper

Combine all ingredients in a small bowl. Serve with crackers.

Curried Mussels

These mussels are also wonderful as a main course over a bed of spinach and jasmine rice. Serves 4

¼ cup (½ stick) unsalted butter
2 tablespoons minced garlic; about 6 cloves
1½ pounds clean mussels in the shell, beards removed
1½ teaspoons curry powder
½ teaspoon kosher salt
several grinds fresh black pepper
½ cup white wine
½ cup heavy cream
½ cup thinly sliced scallions; about 3 scallions

Melt the butter in a medium saucepan over medium-high heat and sauté the garlic for 30 seconds to 1 minute. Add the mussels, curry, salt, and pepper and stir with a wooden spoon. Add the wine and cream and simmer for 5 minutes or until the mussels open. Remove with tongs as each one opens and transfer to a serving bowl. Discard any unopened mussels. When all of the mussels are removed from the pan, pour the pan sauce on top and garnish with the sliced scallions. Serve immediately.

Sun-Dried Tomato Spread

Makes about 2 cups

1 cup sun-dried tomatoes packed in oil
¼ cup lightly packed fresh Italian parsley
¼ cup lightly packed fresh basil
½ cup walnuts
2 ounces grated fresh Romano cheese; about ½ cup lightly packed
2 cloves garlic (or 6 cloves roasted)
several grinds fresh black pepper

Combine all of the ingredients in a food processor and pulse until completely mixed. Refrigerate at least 1 hour before serving; overnight is even better. Serve with Crostini (page 39).

Ducktrap Smoked Mackerel Pâté

Ducktrap is a local company a little to our north which makes wonderful smoked fish. This recipe is also a great way to use up leftover salmon. Serves 4 to 6

4 ounces Ducktrap smoked mackerel
4 ounces cream cheese, room temperature
1 tablespoon grated onion
several grinds fresh black pepper
1 tablespoon diced chives
2 tablespoons fresh lemon juice; about ½ lemon

Combine all ingredients by hand or in a food processor. Refrigerate or serve immediately with French bread or crackers.

Variations
Smoked Trout or Salmon: Replace the smoked mackerel with Ducktrap smoked trout or 1 cup cooked salmon.
Dill: Replace the chives with 1 tablespoon minced dill.
Lime: Replace lemon juice with lime juice.
Horseradish: Add grated horseradish.

Warm Cheddar and Horseradish

A more festive way to serve this dip is to hollow out the center of a round loaf of bread and cut the center into 1-inch cubes. Warm the dip in a double boiler and pour it into the center of the bread and serve with the bread cubes. Serves 4 to 6

4 ounces cream cheese, room temperature
1 tablespoon grated onion
several grinds fresh black pepper
2 tablespoons grated horseradish
1 tablespoon fresh lemon juice
1 tablespoon minced fresh Italian parsley
2 ounces grated cheddar cheese; about ½ cup lightly packed

Preheat oven to 375°F. Combine all the ingredients by hand or in a food processor. Spoon the mixture onto an oven-proof platter. Bake for 20 minutes or until the dip is hot in the center and bubbling around the edges.

Lobster Rangoon

Makes 24

1 cup minced cooked lobster meat; 1 (1-pound) lobster
4 ounces cream cheese, room temperature
$\frac{1}{2}$ teaspoon lemon zest
dash soy sauce
pinch table salt (plus extra for finishing)
several grinds fresh black pepper
8 egg roll wrappers, cut into 4 squares each
peanut oil or other frying oil

Combine the lobster, cream cheese, zest, soy, salt, and pepper in a small bowl. Heat a large stockpot with 2-inches of oil or a fryer to 375°F. Meanwhile, lay out the wrapper squares and place 1 rounded teaspoon of the lobster mixture in the center of each. Pinch the sides together diagonally. Lay some paper towel on top of a platter. Fry the rangoons in 2 batches for 15 to 20 seconds or until golden brown. Remove from the oil to the paper towel and sprinkle with salt.

Parenting at Sea

Some might argue that buying a business and having a baby all in one year would be crazy and we would agree. But we did it. We successfully managed to sail with nearly a full complement of guests our first season and were lucky enough to have Chlöe, a happy baby girl who just liked to be close to Mama and Papa.

Ella arrived a few of years later and for a while, two little ones on board our schooner kept me pretty busy. Now that they are in their teens, they've become an integral part of our business, helping in the galley and on deck, wherever they are needed. Before they were nearly grown, however, we had some notable moments, some of which are chronicled here.

Baby Soup

When Chlöe was two, she liked to sit in the galley and help with dishes. As anyone who has experienced a two-year-old close to water knows, "help" is the last thing you would need if you care about being done with dishes in this century. "Baby Soup" was what we played instead. Chlöe would sit in the big stew pot and we'd "season" her with salt, pepper, and spices, stirring her with the long wooden spoon (of course, this was always the last pot washed). Later this turned into a deck game where we'd give both girls (Ella came three years after Chlöe.) Dixie cups of spices and herbs; some kitchen utensils; and a deck bucket of salt water.

Bunny Overboard

When an errant hat flies off of a guest's head and into the bay, we often take this as an opportunity do an impromptu "man overboard" drill, getting into our stations, rescuing the hat, and recording our rescue time.

When Chlöe was little she had three little stuffed bunnies that she loved to play with. As any parent knows, the loss of a favorite friend is a big deal, and going to some lengths to replace or rescue this friend is worth the effort. One day, one of the bunnies decided to take a trip over the rail. Chlöe was devastated. Jon quickly called "bunny overboard!" and with the help of the guests and crew we retrieved the slightly salty bunny in record time.

Baby as Chart Weight

Ella was one of those babies you could plop down anywhere and she would be happy just looking around. The place she was most happy was the navigation station (where the charts and compass are) right in front of Jon. She ended up acting as a chart weight to keep the charts from blowing away. She'd watch the wheel turn, the GPS screen change, and the flags fly. Now, of course, she doesn't sit still long enough to watch any of that!

Wedding Fairies

The romance of the sea sometimes strikes while on board. There have been numerous engagements, weddings, and renewals of vows on board— all of them special and unique. One year, the girls were asked to be flower girls for an impromptu wedding. They dressed as fairies and scattered flower petals over the deck, grinning from ear to ear the entire time, as the bride walked to her groom.

Kool-Aid® Play Dough

This recipe smells good, but doesn't taste good, so the kids won't eat it. The salt is a preservative, so it will keep for some time if stored in air-tight containers. Different flavors will, of course, give different colors.

2½ cups flour
1 cup table salt
2 packets unsweetened (same color) Kool-Aid®
2 cups boiling water
1 tablespoon canola oil

Combine all the dry ingredients together in a medium-sized bowl. Add the water and mix thoroughly at first with a spoon and then by kneading when the dough has cooled enough to touch.

Guush

The games that the girls played on the boat were often inventive and used what we had on hand, rather than involving a lot of toys. The old adage— the kids want to play with the box more than the toy— was, and still is, true. Guush was an idea a friend gave us and one the girls took to immediately. Both science and play, the surface tension of this mixture causes it to feel like a solid one minute and a liquid the next. Try it and see if you don't want to play with it too!

¾ cup cornstarch
6 tablespoons water
2 to 3 drops food coloring (optional)

Mix 'em all up in a bowl and play.

From the Garden

The lanterns, set out for those nocturnal nature calls, are blown out, and the morning dew wiped from the topsides. My mess cook rises and rubs the fairy dust from her/his eyes and begins the chopping and coffee-making for the day. A counterpoint to the gentle wakening of the guests and crew, this is my busiest time of day. By this time, I'm well into my baking so that most, if not all, is done before breakfast. It's at these times when I think I should wear an apron that says: "Hang on — I'm measuring!"

Roasted Eggplant, Tomato, and Garbanzo Bean Salad

Serves 4 to 6

1 large eggplant
$\frac{1}{4}$ cup fresh lemon juice; about 1 lemon
2 tablespoons balsamic vinegar
$\frac{1}{4}$ cup extra virgin olive oil
$\frac{1}{2}$ teaspoon kosher salt
several grinds fresh black pepper
1 cup minced fresh Italian parsley; about $\frac{1}{2}$ bunch parsley
2 cups diced fresh tomatoes; about 2 tomatoes
2 (16-ounce) cans garbanzo beans, drained

Preheat oven to 400°F. Pierce the skin of the eggplant several times with a fork. Place the whole eggplant in a baking dish and roast it for 20 to 30 minutes or until you can squeeze it and the center is soft. Cut the eggplant in half and set aside to cool slightly. When you can handle it, scoop the flesh out of the skin, and cut it into $\frac{1}{2}$-inch cubes. Whisk together the lemon juice, vinegar, olive oil, salt, and pepper and gently toss the mixture with the eggplant and remaining ingredients and serve.

Black Bean and Grilled Corn Salad

This salad is best if you can grill the corn, though you can use steamed or boiled corn in a pinch. I sometimes roast the corn when we are at a lobster bake — just stick them on a roasting fork and turn them over the fire. You can also use it as a summer salsa for grilled chicken or fish. Serves 4 to 6

4 ears husked corn
2 tablespoons extra virgin olive oil (for the corn and the salad)
1 (15-ounce) can black beans, drained and rinsed
1 tablespoon minced jalapeño pepper, seeds removed
1 cup finely diced red bell pepper; about 1 pepper
$\frac{1}{2}$ cup chopped fresh cilantro
$\frac{1}{4}$ cup diced red onion
$\frac{1}{2}$ teaspoon minced garlic; about 1 small clove
$\frac{1}{2}$ teaspoon kosher salt
several grinds fresh black pepper

Preheat gas or charcoal grill to medium-high heat. Brush the ears of corn with 1 tablespoon olive oil and place the ears directly on the hot grill. Grill for 10 minutes, turning often or until corn is brown in parts and tender. Cool slightly and use a sharp knife to cut the kernels off the cob. Toss the corn with the rest of the ingredients including the remaining 1 tablespoon olive oil in a medium bowl and serve.

Melon and Israeli Couscous Salad

This salad was inspired by a local restaurant. It seems like an odd combination, but I'm always trying the interesting dishes on menus. The tart fruits — grapes and citrus — really give this dish the punch that makes it great. Israeli couscous can be found at a local health food store or at the grocery store in the specialty foods section. Serves 6 to 8

2 cups Israeli couscous
1 cup diced watermelon
1 cup diced honeydew
1 cup diced cantaloupe
1 cup green grapes, cut in half
1 cup currants
1/4 cup canola oil
1 tablespoon lemon zest; about 1 lemon
1/4 cup fresh lemon juice; about 1 lemon
1 tablespoon orange zest; about 1/2 orange
6 tablespoons fresh orange juice; about 1 orange
3 tablespoons fresh lime juice; about 1 lime
1 teaspoon honey
1 tablespoon minced fresh mint
pinch table salt
mint leaves and lemon wedges for garnish

Cook the couscous according to the package directions. Drain and rinse with cold water; set aside. While the couscous is cooking, mix the remaining ingredients together in a large bowl. Toss the drained couscous into the fruit, garnish with mint leaves and citrus wedges and serve.

Sautéed Greens

Serves 4

1 pound greens (spinach, Swiss chard, or dandelion greens are all good)
2 tablespoons extra virgin olive oil
1 teaspoon minced garlic; about 1 clove
2 teaspoons soy sauce
2 teaspoons balsamic vinegar
several grinds fresh black pepper

Destem, wash, and dry the greens well. Coarsely chop. Heat a large skillet over medium-high heat. Add the olive oil and garlic; cook the garlic for 30 seconds. Add the greens, tossing gently, then add the rest of the ingredients and toss again. Cook until the greens are tender. Cooking times will vary depending on the green. Spinach will go the fastest.

Variation
Even More Simple: Omit garlic, soy sauce, and black pepper. Replace the balsamic vinegar with 1 tablespoon lemon juice. Add a pinch of red pepper flakes and salt.

Chicken, Roasted Red Pepper, and Couscous Salad

Serves 4 to 6

3 strips bacon, sliced crosswise
2 cups water
$\frac{1}{2}$ teaspoon kosher salt
1 pound boneless, skinless chicken breasts
1 cup couscous
2 tablespoons extra virgin olive oil
$1\frac{1}{2}$ teaspoons Dijon mustard
1 tablespoon soy sauce
1 tablespoon white wine vinegar
several grinds fresh black pepper
1 large red pepper, roasted, peeled, seeded, and diced
$\frac{1}{4}$ cup thinly sliced scallions
4 ounces baby spinach

Heat a small skillet over medium heat and cook the bacon until crisp. Remove from the pan with a slotted spoon to a paper towel. Bring water and salt to a boil in a medium sauce pan over high heat. Add the chicken and reduce the heat until the liquid is ever so slightly simmering and cook gently for 15 minutes or until just cooked through. Remove the chicken from the pan and set aside to cool. Reserve $1\frac{1}{2}$ cups of the liquid and save the remaining liquid for another recipe. Bring the reserved liquid to a boil and remove from heat. Stir in the couscous, cover, and let it sit for 5 minutes. Meanwhile, whisk the olive oil, mustard, soy sauce, vinegar, and black pepper in a small bowl. Slice the cooled chicken and combine with the vinaigrette mixture, red pepper, scallions, and bacon in a medium bowl. Fluff the couscous with a fork. To plate, layer the spinach, couscous, and then the chicken mixture and serve immediately.

Lentil and Sun-Dried Tomato Salad

For this recipe, I like the greenish-brown French lentils, called Lentilles du Puy, as they are tastier and they don't get mushy as fast. Serves 4

1 cup du Puy or French lentils
$\frac{1}{4}$ cup diced sun-dried tomatoes in oil
$\frac{3}{4}$ cup sliced onion; about 1 small onion
$1\frac{1}{2}$ teaspoon minced fresh oregano
1 cup seeded and finely diced cucumber; about 1 medium cucumber
1 tablespoon extra virgin olive oil
pinch kosher salt
several grinds fresh ground black pepper
2 tablespoons balsamic vinegar
2 tablespoons fresh lemon juice; about $\frac{1}{2}$ lemon
goat or feta cheese for garnish

Bring a medium stockpot of salted water to a boil. Add the lentils and cook for 20 to 25 minutes or until tender. Drain and rinse with cold water. Combine the lentils with the remaining ingredients in a medium bowl. Transfer to a serving platter, garnish with crumbled cheese, and serve.

Roasted Beet and Goat Cheese Salad

Obviously, the fresher the beets, the better the salad, so search for the best. Serves 4 to 6

1 cup whole pecans
1 pound beets, stemmed, scrubbed, and cut into 1-inch wedges
2 tablespoons extra virgin olive oil (for both roasting and finishing)
several pinches kosher salt (for both roasting and finishing)
several grinds fresh black pepper (for both roasting and finishing)
4 ounces crumbled goat cheese; about 1 cup
$\frac{1}{2}$ head romaine lettuce, washed and cut into bite-size pieces
1 tablespoon balsamic vinegar

Preheat oven to 450°F. Place the pecans in a pie pan and toast in the oven for 7 minutes or until fragrant and slightly toasted. Toss the beets with the oil, several pinches of salt, and pepper in a roasting pan. Roast until the beets are tender when pierced with a fork, about 45 minutes to an hour. Set the beets aside to cool slightly and be sure to reserve any excess liquid in the roasting pan. Toss half of the pecans and half of the goat cheese with the lettuce, beets, oil, vinegar, another pinch of salt, and pepper in a large salad bowl. Sprinkle the reserved beet liquid on top of the salad with the rest of the pecans and goat cheese and serve.

Variations
I adapt this recipe to what's available; it's really flexible.
Roasted Onions, Squash, or Beans: Replace the roasted beets with roasted onions, roasted squash, or steamed beans.
Pine Nuts: Replace the pecans with pine nuts or walnuts.
Feta or Blue Cheese: Replace goat cheese with feta or blue cheese.
Lemon: Replace balsamic vinegar with fresh lemon juice.

Social Responsibility

A few years into owning the *J. & E. Riggin*, we made a commitment to the process of social responsibility. I say process, because in any business, balancing social choices with fiscal choices is important. If we are not fiscally responsible and thriving, we are unable to make good choices for the environment or our employees.

In the beginning, we started with things that cost us nothing but made an impact in some way. Recycling and composting became our first goal and while in a home or a land-based restaurant this change of habit might not seem that great, on a boat, the logistics are a challenge. For example, figuring out where to store all of the compost safely without spillage or odor was a considerable head-scratcher. Originally, all of our organic matter went into the municipal dump. Now, each trip we remove at least 5, 5-gallon buckets of vegetable waste which is transferred to our enormous compost pile and eventually feeds our healthy, 3,000 square foot garden. All of the paper waste is either burned as starter in the woodstove or layered in the compost pile including our office paper. Then of course, all of the returnable and recyclable bottles and cans are separated and removed from the waste stream. In the end, the amount of garbage on board decreased from 2 to 3 bags a day to 2 to 3 bags a week and our garden is all the healthier for it.

Our next goal was to find effective and safe cleaning products that didn't pollute the very waters on which we sailed. However, maintaining a very high level of sanitation was and is just as important. Now, there are so many good products on the market, we've switched back to purchasing all of our environmentally-friendly cleaning products. While we haven't found natural alternatives to every product we need to use on the boat, we have seriously reduced the number and amount of non-natural products we use.

Our commitment to buying local produce is one of our stronger decisions and is a cornerstone of my cooking. There are some practical limitations, as Maine's growing season is short and limited, so we supplement what we can't get from our CSA and our own garden at the local grocery store. Over the course of the summer, we work with over 30 local vendors to supply us with the freshest and most Maine produce and products we can source. When we first bought the *Riggin*, so many of these purveyors didn't exist. Now, the chefs in our area have so many choices as small farms, cheesemakers, mushroom foragers, and oyster harvesters all find a market for their hard work on the land or sea.

Lastly, we are conscious about being part of our community in the Maine windjammer fleet, the City of Rockland, and our State of Maine. We consciously look for ways to be responsible, dedicated contributors to the place in which we live and do business. We started slowly, doing what we could, donating what we could. Over time, this ethos became part of our business culture where we share with our guests and our crew how we honor and care for the spaces our business inhabits. We now give 5% of our profits to kids, education, or the environment.

In 2007 we were honored to be one of the first 50 Maine businesses and the first Maine windjammer to receive the Environmental Leader in Hospitality award from Maine's Department of Environmental Protection. It is with pride that we promote eco-tourism for our state and that we are a part of stewarding not only the *Riggin*, but the land and waters on which we ply our trade.

In a Bowl

When the breezes turn brisk or the fog rolls in, there's nothing more soothing than curling chilled hands around a bowl of warm, comforting soup. Leaning in and allowing the steam to rise, warms the cheeks and offers a scent of what is to be savored.

Bermuda Fish Chowder

This stew is enhanced by the addition of two condiments: dark rum and spiced sherry. To make spiced sherry, stuff a whole jalapeño pepper into a small jar or cruet and fill with sherry. Let it sit for at least a day. The spiced sherry will keep for months. Serves 4 to 6

1 tablespoon extra virgin olive oil
1½ cups diced onion; about 1 medium onion
1½ cups peeled and diced carrots; about 2 carrots
1½ cups diced celery; about 2 stalks
1½ cups diced green bell pepper; about 1 pepper
1 tablespoon minced jalapeño pepper; about ½ pepper, seeds removed
3 cups diced yellow-fleshed potatoes; about 2 medium potatoes
2 tablespoons minced garlic; about 6 cloves
2 teaspoons kosher salt
1 (6-ounce) can tomato paste
1 teaspoon ground allspice
¼ teaspoon ground cloves
¼ teaspoon cayenne pepper
3 bay leaves
1 (16-ounce) can diced tomatoes
6 cups clam or fish broth
½ teaspoon Tabasco sauce
½ teaspoon Worcestershire sauce
1 teaspoon fresh lemon juice
1 pound haddock pieces or other white fish
spiced sherry for garnish
dark rum for garnish

Heat the olive oil in a large stockpot over medium-high heat. Add the onion, carrots, celery, and peppers to the pot and sauté for at least 12 minutes or until the vegetables are beginning to sear. Add the potatoes, garlic, salt, tomato paste, and spices and cook for another 5 to 10 minutes. Add the rest of the ingredients except for the fish. Simmer uncovered for 1 hour. Five minutes before serving add the fish and press down to submerge. Stir gently before serving to slightly break up the fish. Serve with a splash of spiced sherry and rum.

Mushroom Barley Soup

Serves 6 to 8

3 tablespoons unsalted butter
2 cups diced onion; about 1 large onion
2 teaspoons minced garlic; about 2 cloves
1 pound button mushrooms, sliced; about 6 cups
½ cup pearled barley
6 cups chicken or vegetable broth
⅓ cup tamari or soy sauce
⅓ cup dry sherry

Melt the butter in a medium stockpot over medium heat. Add the onion and garlic
and sauté for 7 to 10 minutes or until the onion is translucent. Add the mushrooms
and sauté until tender. Add the remaining ingredients and bring the soup to a boil.
Reduce heat to low and simmer for about 20 minutes or until the barley is completely
cooked.

Black Bean Chili

We serve this on the boat with all the fixin's: grated cheddar cheese, chopped onions, sour cream, Pico de Gallo (see below), corn bread, corn chips, salad— the works. It's a bowl extravaganza with a second trip through the lunch line a standard affair. Serves 4 to 6

2 tablespoons canola oil
1 pound ground beef
1 teaspoon kosher salt
2 cups diced onion; about 1 large onion
1 cup diced green bell pepper; about 1 pepper
2 tablespoons minced garlic; about 6 cloves
2 tablespoons ground cumin
2 tablespoons ground chili powder
6 cups beef broth
1 (28-ounce) can diced tomatoes
2 (16-ounce) cans black beans
grated cheddar cheese for garnish
minced onion for garnish
sour cream for garnish

Heat a stockpot over medium heat. Add the oil, ground beef, and salt and cook until browned. Add the onion, pepper, garlic, cumin, and chili powder. Sauté for 7 to 10 minutes or until the onion is translucent. Add the remaining ingredients, reduce heat, and simmer for 1 hour.

Pico de Gallo

This is an easy salsa we make often to serve with either the Black Bean Chili (see above) or the Black Bean and Jasmine Rice Soup (page 67). It's great with both. Makes 2 to 3 cups

3 cups fresh diced tomatoes; about 3 tomatoes
1 tablespoon minced fresh cilantro
3 tablespoons fresh lime juice; about 1 lime
1/2 cup minced onion; about 1 small onion
1 teaspoon minced garlic; about 1 clove
1/2 teaspoon kosher salt
several grinds fresh black pepper
2 tablespoons extra virgin olive oil

Combine all the ingredients in a bowl and serve.

Poached Garlic Soup with Thyme and Red Pepper Cream

Serves 4 to 6

6 heads garlic
2 tablespoons extra virgin olive oil
2 cups diced onion; about 1 large onion
several grinds of fresh black pepper
$^1/_2$ teaspoon table salt
sprig fresh thyme
6 cups chicken broth
1 cup heavy cream

Bring a medium stockpot of salted water to a boil. Meanwhile, break the cloves of garlic apart from the root end. Set aside a large bowl of ice cold water. Add the garlic cloves to the boiling water for one minute. Transfer with a slotted spoon to the ice water. Remove the woody base and the skin from each clove. Heat the oil in a medium stockpot over medium-high heat and add the garlic, onion, salt, pepper, and thyme. Sauté for about 10 minutes or until the onions is translucent. Add the chicken broth and heavy cream and bring to a simmer for 30 minutes. Remove the thyme sprig. Transfer soup in batches to a blender and process carefully with a loose lid, holding a towel over the lid. Serve with Thyme and Red Pepper Cream (see below).

Thyme and Red Pepper Cream

To roast the red pepper over a gas flame, rest the pepper on top of the burner and turn frequently with tongs until the skin becomes charred all over. This takes about 5 minutes total and needs to be watched pretty closely. If you don't have a gas stove, then broil with the same results, turning as above. Remove the pepper to a cutting board and let cool slightly. When you can touch the pepper comfortably, use your thumbs to push the charred skin off the flesh. Remove the core and seeds. Makes about 1 cup

1 cup roasted red pepper, peeled and seeded; about 1 pepper
$^1/_4$ teaspoon table salt
$^1/_2$ teaspoon lemon juice
several grinds of fresh black pepper
$^1/_4$ cup heavy cream

Combine all ingredients in a food processor and blend until it thickens slightly. Use the cream to drizzle on the soup.

Clam Chowder

There are three ingredients that make this a truly traditional chowder: salt pork; day-old biscuits or saltines; and milk The more you substitute, the less traditional your chowder will be. Notice that there is no roux (butter and flour) to thicken the chowder. If there were, then it would be Cream of Clam Soup, not chowder. This recipe calls for evaporated milk. If you are very careful not to bring the chowder to a boil, feel free to substitute regular milk. On the schooner, when I could be called away from the stove at a moment's notice, it's prudent to use evaporated milk, which will not curdle when boiled.
Serves 4 to 6

$^1/_4$ pound salt pork, scored, or 2 strips of bacon, diced
$1^1/_2$ cups diced celery; about 2 stalks
$1^1/_2$ cups diced onion; about 1 medium onion
$1^1/_2$ cups diced white or red-skinned potato (not russets);
    about 1 large potato
$^1/_2$ cup crumbled Saltines or oyster crackers, (it's even better
    if you have day-old biscuits to crumble)
1 (8-ounce) bottle clam juice
2 (10-ounce) cans chopped clams with liquid
1 (14-ounce) can evaporated milk
2 cups water
several grinds fresh black pepper

Heat a medium stockpot over medium-high heat. Add the scored salt pork and render for several minutes. Add the onion and celery and sauté for 7 to 10 minutes or until the vegetables are translucent. Reduce heat to medium, add the potatoes and crackers, and cook for 3 to 5 minutes. Add the clam juice, evaporated milk, water, and pepper. Reduce heat to low and simmer for 1 hour. Add the canned clams and cook another 2 minutes before serving..

Variations
Whole Clam: Replace the canned clams with 1 pound of clams in the shell. Before starting the chowder, place the clams in cold, salted water and sprinkle them with cornmeal. Leave the clams to soak while you prepare the rest of the chowder. When the chowder is ready, rinse the clams and add them to the pot. When the clams open, about 5 minutes, the chowder is ready to serve. Serve immediately.

Salmon and Corn: Replace the canned clams with 1 pound of fresh, skinned, boneless salmon. Cut the kernels off two ears of corn. Add the cobs when you add the clam juice and water; simmer 1 hour. Remove the cobs. Five minutes before serving add the salmon and corn kernels. Press down to submerge. Stir gently before serving to slightly break up the fish.

Haddock: Replace the canned clams with 1 pound of fresh, boneless haddock. Five minutes before serving add the haddock and press down to submerge. Stir gently before serving to slightly break up the fish.

Leek and Lobster: Replace 1 cup onions with 1 cup leeks. Replace canned clams with 2 (1¼-pound) lobsters. Steam the lobsters for 8 minutes or until their shells are bright red. Remove the lobsters to a bowl to cool. Reserve all of the lobster liquid. When the lobsters are cool enough to work with, remove the meat from the shells and pour the excess liquid back into the pot. Use this in place of the clam juice in the recipe. Cut the meat into ½-inch pieces and add just before serving.

On top of any of these fancier chowders you could serve non-traditional garnishes such as minced scallions, minced fresh herbs, crème fraîche (or sour cream), or home-made croutons.

Tomato Soup with Herbed Yogurt

Serves 4 to 6

Soup
1 tablespoon extra virgin olive oil
2 cups diced onion; about 1 large onion
1 tablespoon minced garlic; about 3 cloves
2 tablespoons orange zest; about $1/2$ orange
3 tablespoons fresh orange juice; about $1/2$ orange
1 tablespoon dried basil
1 tablespoon dried marjoram
1 tablespoon dried cumin
$1/4$ teaspoon red pepper flakes
2 (28-ounce) cans crushed tomatoes
$1 1/2$ cups chicken or vegetable broth
1 square (1 ounce) bittersweet chocolate

Herbed Yogurt
$1/2$ cup plain yogurt
$1/4$ cup thinly sliced scallions; about 1 scallion
$1 1/2$ tablespoons minced fresh basil
1 teaspoon minced garlic; about 1 clove

Soup
Heat a stockpot over medium-high heat and add the olive oil, onion, garlic, orange zest, orange juice, and spices. Sauté for 7 to 10 minutes or until the onion is translucent. Add the rest of ingredients and simmer for 1 hour.

Herbed Yogurt
Meanwhile whisk the yogurt ingredients together in a small bowl. Serve the soup with a dollop of herbed yogurt.

Spinach Gorgonzola Soup

Serves 4 to 6

2 tablespoons unsalted butter
2 cups diced onion; about 1 large onion
2 tablespoons minced garlic; about 6 cloves
$1/2$ teaspoon kosher salt
several grinds fresh black pepper

2 sprigs fresh thyme

4 ounces crumbled Gorgonzola cheese; about 1 cup

4 cups chicken or vegetable broth

5 ounces spinach, washed and julienned; about 4 cups lightly packed

2 cups peeled, seeded, and diced tomatoes; about 2 tomatoes

Melt the butter in a stockpot over medium-high heat. Add the onion, garlic, salt, pepper, and thyme and cook until the onion is translucent. Add the Gorgonzola and chicken broth and bring the broth to a simmer. Transfer the soup in batches to a blender and process carefully with a loose lid, holding a towel over the lid. Place the spinach in the stockpot and cook for 1 minute. Add the tomatoes and puréed soup, bring to a simmer, and serve.

Black Bean and Jasmine Rice Soup

We often serve this soup with Pico de Gallo (page 62). Serves 4 to 6

2 tablespoons extra virgin olive oil

2 cups diced onion; about 1 large onion

1 cup diced green bell pepper; about 1 pepper

1 dried Ancho chili, reconstituted and minced

2 tablespoons minced garlic; about 6 cloves

1 tablespoon ground cumin

1 teaspoon kosher salt

1 (14-ounce) can diced tomatoes

1 (16-ounce) can black beans

5 cups chicken or vegetable broth

3 tablespoons fresh lime juice; about 1 lime

$1/2$ cup jasmine rice

sour cream for garnish

lime wedges for garnish

coarsely chopped fresh cilantro leaves for garnish

Heat the olive oil in a medium stockpot over medium-high heat. Add the onion, peppers, garlic, cumin, and salt to the pot and sauté for 7 to 10 minutes or until the onion is translucent. Add the remaining ingredients except for the rice and simmer for 45 minutes. Add the jasmine rice and simmer for another 15 minutes. Add additional broth or water if needed. Garnish with sour cream, lime wedges, and cilantro.

Thai Red Curry Soup

Serves 4 to 6

1 cup white wine
bottom 4 inches of 2 fresh lemon grass stalks, thinly sliced
$\frac{1}{2}$ tablespoon julienned peeled fresh ginger
1 teaspoons minced garlic; about 1 clove
2 cups bottled clam juice
1 (16-ounce) can unsweetened coconut milk
1 teaspoon red curry paste
$\frac{1}{2}$ teaspoon lime zest
$1\frac{1}{2}$ tablespoons cornstarch
1 tablespoon water
2 tablespoons thinly sliced fresh basil
$\frac{1}{2}$ tablespoon fresh lemon juice
6 ounces snapper fillet, cut into $\frac{1}{2}$-inch cubes
12 medium uncooked shrimp, peeled, deveined, and halved

Combine the wine, lemongrass, ginger, and garlic in a large, heavy-duty saucepan.
Bring to a boil over medium-high heat. Add the clam juice and coconut milk and
simmer about 15 minutes. Stir in the curry paste and lime peel. Mix the cornstarch
and water in small bowl until smooth. Add to the soup and bring to a boil, stirring
often. Reduce heat and simmer 5 minutes, stirring occasionally. Add the basil, lemon
juice, fish, and shrimp; simmer about 2 minutes or just until the fish is cooked through.

Turnip and Leek Soup

*I created this soup to deal with a mountain of turnips that we received from Hope's Edge Farm.
It reminds me of potato and leek soup — just a tasty twist on a classic.* Serves 4 to 6

2 tablespoons unsalted butter
2 cups diced onion; about 1 large onion
3 cups cleaned and diced leeks; about 2 leeks
6 cups peeled and diced turnips; about 4 turnips
2 teaspoons kosher salt
1 teaspoon freshly grated nutmeg
$1\frac{1}{2}$ tablespoons grated fresh ginger
1 cup white wine
2 cups vegetable broth
1 cup sour cream for garnish

Melt the butter in a large stockpot over medium-high heat. Add everything but the wine, broth, and sour cream and sauté for 7 to 10 minutes or until the onion is translucent. Add the wine and broth and simmer for at least 30 minutes. For a more rustic soup, leave it as it is; to fancy it up a bit, whiz everything in the blender. Garnish with a dollop of sour cream.

Italian Sausage Soup

Sometimes I have leftover roasted garlic and I use it in place of the fresh garlic. If you have an herb garden like I do, then by all means use fresh herbs in place of the dried. Serves 4 to 6

2 tablespoons extra virgin olive oil
1 pound sweet Italian sausage, cut into ¹/₂-inch slices
   (or hot if you want a spicier soup)
2 cups diced onion; about 1 large onion
2 tablespoons minced garlic; about 6 cloves
1 teaspoon kosher salt
several grinds fresh black pepper
2 teaspoons dried oregano
2 teaspoons dried marjoram
2 teaspoons dried thyme
2 teaspoons dried basil
2 cups diced zucchini; about 1 zucchini
2 cups diced summer squash; about 1 squash
4 cups peeled and diced red-skinned or white potatoes;
   about 2 large potatoes
1 cup red wine
1 (14-ounce) can diced tomatoes
4 to 5 cups chicken broth
¹/₂ cup heavy cream (optional)
2 cups chopped spinach or kale

Heat the olive oil in a medium stockpot over medium-high heat. Add the sausage and sauté until brown. Add the onion, garlic, salt, pepper, and herbs and sauté for 7 to 10 minutes or until the onion is translucent. Add the zucchini and summer squash and sauté for another 5 minutes. Add the potatoes, wine, tomatoes, broth, and optional cream and bring to a boil. Reduce heat to low and simmer for 45 minutes adding more broth if needed. If you are using spinach, add it and cook another minute or two. If you are using kale, add it and cook for an additional 15 minutes.

 # History

From the 1880s through the 1930s oystering was a national industry with thriving centers on the East and West Coasts. At the turn of the century, oysters were the chief fishery product of the United States. The most common American vessel type was the two-masted schooner. Tens of thousands of these vessels were built and operated in the heyday of oystering and fishing.

There are now only a few oyster schooners known to survive in the United States, the *J. & E. Riggin* is the youngest of the surviving oyster schooners and is an outstanding representative of the late and final form of oyster schooner, representing the introduction of modern naval architectural theory and design.

The harvesting and later the cultivation of the oyster was one of the earliest fisheries industries in North America. Colonial interest in oystering led to widespread and intensive harvesting, and ultimately, by the 18th century, to government efforts to regulate the industry and conserve and nurture oyster beds. Oyster cultivation began in the 1820s, and gradually reinvigorated a flagging industry at a time when demand for oysters was increasing. As early as 1800, "the widespread desire for oysters on the half shell at home or in public eating places kept the shell trade alive." A century later, oysters were "the chief fishery product of the United States and the most extensively eaten of all shellfish ....Everyone, especially those living along the shore, knew all about this wholesome, nutritious bivalve and the multimillion dollar industry it spawned."

After a half-century in service, including time as a motor powered vessel, the *Riggin* was restored to her sailing rig by Dave and Sue Allen and placed in service as a "Maine Windjammer," in 1977, carrying passengers in commercial recreational service as part of a "dude fleet" that dates to the 1930s. They owned the boat for twenty-four years before selling her to Jon and me in 1998.

Photos: Charles Riggin (top left), Jacob Riggin (top right), Edward Riggin (bottom left), Walter Wardley (bottom right)

The *Riggin* has a rich history, but one of her claims to fame was written about in *Under Sail: The Dredgeboats of Delaware Bay* by Donald H. Rolfs. This sums up her history and her character nicely.

"Undoubtedly, the most legendary schooner that ever sailed the bay was the *J and E Riggin*. This dredgeboat was 76 feet, 4 inches long with a 22 foot, 3 inch beam. The *J and E* was polish rigged and carried 4000 square feet of canvas. Captain Ed Riggin involuntarily glows from stem to stern as he relates the exploits of the grand old boat. "My gosh," he said," it was almost as if she was a live creature a-risin' up out o' the sea, runnin' before the wind, a-goin' wing and wing. I would have to climb up on top of the wheel box to see where I was goin'. You know, she was never beat in a race. Many of the 'old gents' thought they could take her but nobody ever did. Sunday afternoons they used to wait for us at the mouth of the river to give her a try, but there weren't nobody could ever take her."

Captain Frank Hinson concurred with Captain Riggin's estimation of the *J and E* "I believe it was the way she was rigged up," said Captin Frank. "She was hung just right. We were comin' down the bay one day and I had the *Richard Lore*, an old time boat, pushin' down with the yawlboat... there wasn't a bit of wind, not a bit, to plant... looked up and here come the *J and E Riggin* down the bay. She was comin' on so fast we thought she was pushin' with a yawlboat. She went by us and didn't even have her yawlboat down! She had a line from her main boom to the rigging on one side and line from her fore boom to the rigging on the other side... had her wung out... and that thing was a-goin' down the bay just the same as us. Yep, she was hung just exactly right... take a little breeze of wind and you would just have to reef her down to nothing to hold her dredges on the bottom."

The *J. & E. Riggin* is still a beautiful schooner and although she's still fast, she doesn't carry oysters anymore, she carries passengers. She was built as an oystering schooner in 1927 in Dorchester, New Jersey on the Maurice River. Charles Riggin, a fisherman, had her built and named her after his two sons Jacob and Edward. She gained a fine reputation in the Delaware Bay as an able sailor, winning the only Oyster Schooner Race ever held in 1929. She was designated a National Historic Landmark in 1991.

Over the next two decades, the Riggin boys and their father took turns at the helm oystering off the coast of New Jersey. Our family now carries on the tradition of a family run business. Originally, we chose to own a Maine windjammer because we could raise our children together on board. We are lucky to be following in Charles Riggin's footsteps and be able to raise our daughters in such a unique way.

At a Glance

1927 – Built at Stowaman's Shipyard in Dorchester, New Jersey for Capt. Charles Riggin, named after his two sons, Jacob and Edward.

1929 – Wins the only Oyster Schooner Race.

1960 – Changes hands from the Riggin family to Capt. Walter Wardley who converts her to ground fishing vessel in New York.

1977 – Capt. Dave & Sue Allen of Rockland, Maine buy the worn schooner and convert her for passenger sail.

1991 – The National Park Service designates the *J. & E. Riggin* as a National Historic Landmark.

1998 – Capts. Jon Finger & Anne Mahle become the new stewards of the *J. & E.*

2007 – Wins the state of Maine's Environmental Leader Award –one of the first 50 businesses and the first Maine windjammer.

Creative Kitchen

Tools For Inspired Cooks

Most recipes do not stand on their own, but are enhanced by the other dishes with which they are combined. Those who need exact recipes to do their cooking work should simply enjoy this window into a different way of thinking about how recipes can connect with each other. Those who wish to explore—have at it and don't stop here!

Buttermilk Pancakes	*with* Riggin Ham + poached eggs + steamed asparagus	*with* scrambled eggs + roasted kale + cheddar	*with* fried egg + salami
Roasted Mushroom and Artichoke Sauce	*on* Oven-Baked Polenta	*with* Risotto	*over* Sautéed Greens
New England Boiled Dinner	*on* soft dinner rolls + sauerkraut + mustard	*in* Strata	*in* hash
Sautéed Greens	*in* poached eggs + cheese + avocado	*over* black beans + cheese + salsa	*over* Cinnamon Roasted Sweet Potatoes + walnuts
Sage and Rosemary Pork Loin with Cranberry Port Sauce	*on* focaccia + slaw + Havarti	*with* Sautéed Greens	*in* hash
Bolognese Sauce	*in* lasagna	*over* baked stuffed shells	*over* Oven-Baked Polenta
German Apple Pancake	*in* maple ricotta	*with* Mocha Syrup	*with* bacon + cheddar
Fruit Compote	*in* sticky buns	*on* Three-Grain Pan- cakes + yogurt	*with* maple syrup + ice cream
Shirred Eggs	*with* fresh corn + salsa	*with* crème fraîche + herbs	*with* sausage + roasted tomatoes

Green Olive Tapenade

with
roasted red peppers + provolone + Italian bread

in
Crusty Peasant Bread

on
Focaccia + sliced tomatoes

Herbed Feta Cheese

on
pasta + toasted pine nuts

heated
under broiler

in
pita + hummus + micro greens

Crêpes

with
Riggin Ham + spinach + Gruyère

with
Lobster Dip + asparagus

with
Salmon + dill + crème fraîche

Pico de Gallo

with
Salmon

with
sour cream + chips

over
black beans + rice

Chicken Paprika

with
Oven-Baked Polenta + Sautéed Greens

with
Annie's Mashed Potatoes

with
egg noodles + sour cream

Curried Mussels

on
pasta + tomatoes

over
rice + cilantro + fried garlic

over
couscous

Sun-Dried Tomato Spread

on
pasta + Parmesan + chicken

on
Focaccia

in
Poached Garlic Soup

Thyme and Red Pepper Cream

with
Roasted 5-Herb Chicken

with
Pork Tenderloin

with
Sage, Rosemary, and Salt-Rubbed Roast Pork Loin

Potato Pancakes

with
poached eggs + Pico de Gallo

with
Shirred Eggs

in
Roasted 5-Herb Chicken

Riggin Ham

with
Cheddar Cheese Biscuits + pickles

with
Zucchini and Goat Cheese Gratin

in
Frittata

Mocha Syrup

in
a cocktail + cream + rum

on
ice cream + pecans

in
banana trifle

On the Side

Fresh vegetables arrive at the dock from our farmer and are wheeled down the ramp in boxes to be loaded in the galley. The boxes overflow with the tips of leeks and the ruffles of lettuce. The smell of earth and green mingles with the ever-present scent of the ocean and with that our shore and our sea life are comingled.

Cheesy Potatoes

Our crew calls this recipe "cheesy potatoes," but it's really a classic potato gratin. I serve this with Riggin *Ham (page 113).* Serves 4 to 6

1 teaspoon unsalted butter
2 pounds yellow-fleshed or russet potatoes; about 4 medium potatoes
2 cups whipping or heavy cream
1 cup chicken broth
1 teaspoon kosher salt
several grinds fresh black pepper
$\frac{1}{4}$ teaspoon freshly grated nutmeg
2 whole cloves garlic
2 ounces finely shredded Gruyère, Emmenthaler, or Comté cheese;
    about 1 cup lightly packed

Preheat the oven to 400°F. Lightly grease a 9- x 13-inch baking dish. Using a very sharp knife or mandolin, carefully cut the potatoes into $\frac{1}{8}$-inch slices. Bring everything except the cheese to a boil in a large, heavy saucepan over medium-high heat. Stir occasionally and very gently so you don't break up the potato slices. Add any additions here (see below). When the cream boils, pour the mixture into the prepared baking dish; remove the garlic cloves and shake the dish to settle the potato slices. Sprinkle the cheese evenly over the potatoes. Bake until the top is deep golden brown, the cream has thickened, and the potatoes are extremely tender when pierced with a knife, about 40 to 45 minutes. Don't worry if the dish looks too liquid at this point; it will set up as it cools a bit, about 15 minutes.

Variations
Scallion and Roasted Red Pepper: Add 1 cup thinly sliced scallions and 1 cup sliced roasted red pepper.
Blue Cheese and Walnut: Replace cheese with 4 ounces blue cheese and 1 cup chopped walnuts.
Thyme and Onion: Add large sprig of thyme to the heavy cream and then 2 cups thinly sliced onions when the potatoes are added.
Jalapeño and Jack: Add 1 tablespoon minced jalapeño pepper and 2 cups diced fresh tomatoes. Replace the Gruyère cheese with Monterey Jack.
No Cream and Onion: Add 2 cups thinly sliced onion when the potatoes are added. Replace the cream with extra chicken broth.

Zucchini, Sage, and Goat Cheese Gratin

Serves 4 to 6

1 pound of zucchini, sliced into $\frac{1}{4}$-inch slices; about 3 zucchinis
3 tablespoons extra virgin olive oil
$\frac{1}{2}$ teaspoon kosher salt
several grinds of fresh black pepper
$\frac{1}{2}$ cup breadcrumbs
1 teaspoon minced garlic; about 1 clove
1 ounce crumbled goat cheese; about $\frac{1}{4}$ cup
3 sage leaves, julienned

Preheat oven to 400°F. Layer the zucchini in a 9- x 13-inch pan in 4 overlapping long rows. Drizzle each row with olive oil and sprinkle with salt and pepper. Combine the rest of the ingredients in a small bowl and spread over the zucchini evenly. Bake for 40 to 50 minutes or until the zucchini is cooked all the way though and the cheese begins to brown.

Annie's Mashed Potatoes

I've used olive oil in these potatoes as well. It's a great way to lower the fat content — or as a substitute if you find yourself in the middle of Penobscot Bay with very little butter left for the week (oops!).
Serves 4

2 pounds yellow-fleshed potatoes, peeled and quartered;
    about 4 medium potatoes
$1/4$ cup ($1/2$ stick) unsalted butter
$1/2$ cup whole milk
1 teaspoon table salt
pinch white pepper

Place the potatoes in a medium stockpot and cover with cold, salted water. Bring the water to a boil over high heat. Reduce the heat and simmer for 20 minutes or until the potatoes are tender when poked with a fork. Drain the water and add the remaining ingredients. Mash the potatoes with either a potato ricer or with a mixer. Add more milk if necessary and test for salt and pepper.

Variations
Garlic: Add 1 whole head of peeled garlic cloves to the stockpot with the potatoes.
Olive Oil: Replace the butter with extra virgin olive oil.
Goat Cheese and Dill: Replace yellow-fleshed potatoes with russet potatoes. Add 6 ounces crumbled goat cheese and $1^1/2$ teaspoons minced fresh dill. Reduce the butter to 2 tablespoons.

Roasted Parsnips with Paprika

Serves 4 to 6

$1^1/2$ pounds parsnips; about 6 parsnips
2 tablespoons extra virgin olive oil
$1/4$ teaspoon kosher salt
$1/4$ teaspoon paprika
several grinds of fresh black pepper

Preheat the oven to 450°F. Peel the parsnips and cut into $1/2$-inch sticks, removing any center woody portions. On a baking sheet with sides, toss the parsnips with olive oil, salt, paprika, and pepper. Roast in the oven for 20 minutes or until the edges begin to brown and the centers are tender.

Roasted Red Wine Potatoes

These are Jon's all-time favorite potatoes. I serve them with the Roasted Pork Loin (page 110).
Serves 4 to 6

$1^1/_2$ pounds red-skinned potatoes cut into 1-inch pieces;
    6 to 8 medium potatoes
2 teaspoons kosher salt
several grinds fresh black pepper
1 whole head garlic, peeled
2 cups red wine
$^1/_2$ cup heavy cream

Preheat oven to 375°F. Put all the ingredients except the cream into a 9- x 13-inch
baking dish. Bake for 1 hour, stirring once or twice. Add cream and bake for another
10 minutes or until the potatoes are tender and the liquid has reduced and thickened.

Potato Pancakes

Makes 8 to 12 pancakes

$^1/_2$ cup grated onion; about 1 small onion
2 pounds yellow-fleshed potatoes, peeled and grated;
    about 4 medium potatoes
1 teaspoon table salt
several grinds fresh black pepper
1 large egg white
3 tablespoons unsalted butter
sour cream for garnish

Place the onion and potatoes in a strainer and press out as much moisture as possible.
Combine all the ingredients except the butter and sour cream in a medium bowl.
Heat a skillet over medium heat and add a tablespoon of butter. Drop spoonfuls of
the potato mixture onto the skillet and flatten gently with the back of the spoon. Cook
for 5 minutes on each side or until browned and cooked through. Add more butter
to the pan if needed. Repeat until all of the potato mixture is cooked. Serve with
sour cream.

Rosemary Potatoes

Serves 4

4 russet potatoes, peeled
3 sprigs of rosemary
$^1/_4$ cup extra virgin olive oil
$1^1/_2$ teaspoons kosher salt
several grinds fresh black pepper

Preheat oven to 375°F. Cut the potatoes into $^1/_4$-inch thick slices, being careful to not slice them through completely. Insert a few rosemary leaves between each slice. Rub with the olive oil, salt, and pepper and place in an 8-inch baking pan. Bake for 1 hour or until the potatoes are tender.

Yorkshire Pudding

This is a classic that I often serve with Riggin *Rib Roast (page 106)*. Serves 6 to 8 or makes 12 popovers

1 cup all-purpose flour
$^1/_2$ teaspoon table salt
several grinds fresh black pepper
2 large eggs
$1^1/_2$ cups whole milk
drippings from roast beef (substitute olive oil or bacon fat)

Preheat oven to 450°F. Sift the dry ingredients into a medium bowl. Make a well in the center and whisk in the eggs and the milk, gradually incorporating the flour. Cover and refrigerate 30 minutes. Meanwhile, heat a 9-inch cast-iron skillet or a popover pan in the oven until the skillet is very hot. Add drippings to the skillet and immediately pour in the batter. Bake uncovered, about 25 to 30 minutes (less if using the popover pan). The pudding is done when it's puffy, golden brown, and crispy. Serve immediately.

Variation
Popovers: Heat a 12-cup popover pan in the oven until very hot. Add drippings to each well and pour in the batter. Reduce baking time to 15 to 20 minutes. If serving immediately, make a slit in the side to release steam and serve. If baking ahead, return to the oven for another 5 minutes.

Oven-Baked Polenta

Serves 4 to 6

1 cup medium-coarse or coarse cornmeal (preferably organic
    stone-ground)
4 cups chicken or vegetable broth, or 2 cups each water and whole milk
1 tablespoon unsalted butter or extra virgin olive oil
1 teaspoon kosher salt

Preheat the oven to 350°F. Combine all the ingredients a 3-quart oven-proof
skillet. Bake, uncovered, for 40 minutes (the mixture will separate and take more
than half the cooking time to come together). Remove the skillet from the oven and
let the polenta rest in the pan for 5 minutes before serving.

Variations
Bright Green Kale Polenta: Puree a big handful of kale with Parmesan, extra virgin
olive oil, garlic, sea salt, black pepper until the consistency of pesto. Cook the polenta
and then swirl in at the end.
Bacon and Fontina: Render 3 strips of minced bacon, drain the fat, and add to the
polenta. Sprinkle with 1 cup grated Fontina.
Fried Polenta: Cook and chill the polenta overnight in a 9- x 9-inch pan. Cut into
9 pieces and pan-fry in a non-stick skillet with olive oil until both sides are golden
brown. Sprinkle with cheese.

Cinnamon Roasted Sweet Potatoes

Serves 4 to 6

3 tablespoons unsalted butter
1 teaspoon ground cinnamon
2 or 3 large sweet potatoes, cut in half lengthwise
1/2 teaspoon kosher salt
several grinds fresh black pepper

Preheat oven to 375°F. Melt the butter and the cinnamon in a small saucepan. Place
the potatoes in a baking pan and toss with the melted butter and cinnamon mixture.
Sprinkle with salt and pepper and roast for 1 hour, until the potatoes are tender.

Roasted Butternut Squash and Tomatoes with Farmer's Cheese

Serves 4 to 6

1 pound butternut squash, peeled, seeded and cut into 1-inch chunks;
    about 4 cups
2 tomatoes, cut into at least 8 wedges each; about 3 cups
1/4 cup extra virgin olive oil
1 teaspoon kosher salt
several grinds fresh black pepper
4 ounces crumbled farmer's cheese; about 1 cup
2 cups lightly packed spinach leaves

Preheat oven to 400°F. Toss the squash and tomatoes separately with olive oil, salt, and pepper on a baking sheet with sides. Roast the tomatoes for 30 to 35 minutes or until the edges begin to brown. Remove them from the pan and continue roasting the squash until it begins to brown on the edges and is completely cooked through, about another 20 to 30 minutes. To serve, lay spinach leaves on a platter and top with the roasted tomatoes and then the squash and farmer's cheese. Serve immediately. This recipe is delicious served with Lemon Risotto (page 85).

Risotto

Serves 4 to 6

2 tablespoons unsalted butter
1 cup diced onion; about 1 medium onion
2 cups Arborio rice
1/3 cup white wine
4 to 5 cups low-salt chicken broth
1/4 teaspoon kosher salt
pinch of white pepper
1 ounce grated Parmesan cheese; about 1/2 cup lightly packed

In a medium saucepan, melt the butter over medium heat. Add the onion and sauté for 10 minutes or until translucent. If the onion begins to brown, reduce heat to medium low. Add the rice and stir for one minute. Add the salt, pepper, wine, and 1 cup of the broth and stir. Bring to a simmer and wait until the liquid is absorbed before adding more broth. Continue to add the broth, one cup at a time, as needed, stirring frequently. The rice is done when the liquid is completely incorporated and the grains are just the tiniest bit al dente in the center. Add Parmesan cheese and serve.

Variations
Lemon Risotto: Add 1 teaspoon lemon zest; zest from about 1 lemon. Add 2 tablespoons lemon juice; juice from about 1/2 of a lemon.
Barley Risotto: Add 1 cup diced celery with the onions. Replace the Arborio rice with barley.
Green Pea Risotto: Add 2 cups fresh peas. Puree half the peas in a blender with hot broth. Add just enough to achieve a smooth paste or a little looser. Reserve the remaining broth for the rice. Add the pureed peas and the other half of the fresh peas to the risotto just before serving.

A Week At Sea

It's just before boarding on Sunday night; the crew does a few last minute touches of polish on the brass, one more check of the deck to make sure all the lines are flemished and coiled, and at 5 p.m. the first guests begin to arrive. Some are first-time guests, other are repeat guests who return every year, all are welcomed warmly. One returning couple tells us that their trip on the *Riggin* starts when they get in the car to leave their home— off come the watches and they don't go back on until we hit the dock after a week onboard.

Everyone stows their gear in their cabins, then are shown around the deck and galley by one of our crew. They pause to help themselves to hot coffee or tea and homemade cookies, then start meeting their fellow guests and crew. I'm meeting guests as I arrange the flowers I've just pick from the garden behind our house. A harbor seal pops his head up, eyeing the scene curiously.

At 6 p.m. Captain Jon gathers everyone 'round for "captain's call"— introducing the ins and outs of shipboard living and talking about what to expect for the week. Except for the hottest days of the summer, the woodstove is a welcome source of heat in the evening as the air cools; folks gather in the varnished pine galley to read, knit, play games, or get to know each other.

Monday
Too excited to sleep, most everyone's up early Monday morning. The crew is bucketing down the decks, packing ice and loading wood. A week's worth of provisions is carefully loaded and packed, arranged in the order of when it will be used. I've been up since 4:30 a.m., coffee is ready and on deck by 7 a.m. After a hearty breakfast of pancakes and bacon, guests go ashore for any last minute items they've forgotten— foul weather gear, sunscreen, soda, wine, and beer.

Breakfast is over and cleaned up. Some folks, already eager to help, work with the crew to take down the awning and prepare the *Riggin* for departure. Finally, it's time. We cast off lines, everyone helps to raise the sails, and we're off. The moment that the sails are raised and the yawl boat engine is turned off there seems to be a collective sigh— of relief, happiness, peace. A favorite place on the boat once the sails are up is at the bow; one guest of ours can always be found there at this time "clearing my head". There's a joy to being back out on the bay— our motto at this point is, "If we don't have it, we don't need it."

We aren't alone— other windjammers are leaving their homeports as well. It's a majestic sight. As we pass both the Rockland and Owl's Head Lighthouses and look south across the sparkling water, all we can see is open space, sky, and water. To the north and west are the legendary Camden Hills and all of the splendid islands of Penobscot Bay. The breeze is brisk so we have time to play. As we race up to Camden to see the boats entering the bay, we're feeling the wind on our cheeks, the exciting motion of the schooner, and the sound of the waves lapping against the bow.

After a magical first day, we ghost into Bucks Harbor. A talented steel band frequently performs by the general store and tonight is no exception. After dinner, we all go ashore to explore, walk around, and listen to the music. Robert McCloskey wrote about Bucks Harbor in his renowned children's book *One Morning in Maine*. He was a two-time Caledcott medalist— *Make Way for Ducklings* won in 1942 and *Time of Wonder* in 1958. He also wrote *Blueberries for Sal*, our family's favorite.

Tuesday

It's a sunny morning; and this is the warmest harbor we will be in all week long. My girls know it— so they talk me into going for a swim. This convinces a few sturdy folks to also give it a try. Some are in and out— you almost wonder if they got wet! Others discover that it's refreshing and stay in to swim around the boat and maybe wash their hair (we have a shower onboard but many guests still prefer to wash with natural seawater). While we are swimming, the crew is busy readying the boat for sailing. This is the first morning we raise the anchor— it's all done by hand and is a real team effort! What satisfaction to sail off the anchor under sail through the efforts of those on board.

It's one of those meandering days, so we turn southwest to head down Eggemoggin Reach. There is a high suspension ridge that connects Little Deer Island to the mainland. We sail under it calling "ollie, ollie oxen free!" Once, we saw three deer here— swimming from the mainland to Little Deer Island. Folks settle in fairly quickly today, finding a favorite spot on a cabin top for reading, or on the bowsprit quietly looking out to sea. Many are on the quarterdeck by the wheel, listening to Captain Jon answer questions and tell a few stories.

After a leisurely day, we find ourselves anchored in Burnt Coat Harbor on Swan's Island, a snug and pretty harbor that boasts a historic lighthouse and residents that can trace their family roots back to the Boston Tea Party. Jon pulls out his guitar and soon we're singing favorite songs of the sea and of the ships and people that make the ocean their home.

Wednesday

Wanting to explore a bit, several of us go ashore and walk out to Burnt Coat Harbor Light on Hockamock Head, admiring wildflowers and seashells on our route. We take pictures and leave the wildflowers and seashells for others to appreciate as well. Back on the boat, we sing to raise the sails, the cadence is easy to adopt and the sails go up quickly. I am in our yawl boat, Black Beauty, pushing the schooner out of the harbor. Jon built her out of local oak, cedar, brown heart, and silver baly. She is our tugboat and our launch; she helps us get where we need to go when we don't have enough wind and ferries us ashore for walks and shopping.

Wednesdays are one of my favorite days of the week. It's on this day that shoulders relax, laughter is easy, conversations meaningful, and even moments of silence are noted and appreciated. There is a simpler appreciation of our surroundings. This day is the turning point as the magic and the slower tempo of being on Penobscot Bay really seeps in and the hectic pace of our lives on shore falls away.

By late afternoon we've dropped the "hook" (anchor) in Stonington. Lobster boats cluster around the harbor and houses seem to protect the hill. This is a true lobstering village. From the deck we can see one building painted with huge letters, spelling out "Opera House". It's nearly time for dinner, but there'll be plenty of time to go ashore tomorrow. After smelling dinner all afternoon long, we finally get a taste. All hands sit in a galley made cozy by the light of kerosene lanterns and fresh flowers on the table.

Thursday

It's early morning, but excitement starts to build as Capt. Jon returns from an early trip in the yawl boat with a crate full of fresh lobsters. After breakfast, Black Beauty ferries us ashore to Stonington, a town located on the southern tip of Deer Island which is aptly named. There is abundant evidence in town and on the surrounding islands of the granite quarries that were a mainstay for the town in the 19th century. Nowadays, the residents of Stonington earn a living from lobstering and a few craft shops.

Jan and Evelyn Kok were a feature of Stonington for years. The oldest kids we knew, and a magical couple, they welcomed and entertained windjammer passengers for decades in their tiny, eclectic shop along the harbor. Both were artists— Jan a music director and Evelyn an illustrator. Their shop was full of fascinating artwork and knick-knacks. Very little of it is for sale, but Evelyn made beautiful bookmarks featuring all the schooners as well as a number of beautiful line drawings. It was wonderful to poke around while Evelyn hand-lettered guests' names on the bookmarks. It was not at all unusual for Jan and Evelyn to break into one of their songs— it felt like you'd walked into a pixie's tea party!

After a leisurely morning ashore, we weigh anchor, raise sails, and we're off, cruising among the islands of Merchant's Row. We see a pod of porpoise appear among the waves— cameras and binoculars are quickly pulled out. We anchor early near a sandy beach for our lobster bake. There's no rush as we have plenty of time to explore the island before we settle down to all the lobster we can eat. The last boatload of guests return to the *Riggin* at dusk. We got a little extra sun today and everyone is happy and full. We watch as the stars come out and have an impromptu star-gazing session, picking out the Big and Little Dipper, Cassiopeia, and the Summer Triangle.

Friday

As the week goes by, everyone relaxes more and more and rises later and later. But coffee is till ready at 7 a.m. for early risers, and several guests take our peapod out for a quiet row.

By Friday, everyone is an ol' salt and is ready to help get the *Riggin* underway. The Captain calls "Heave out!" and "Set your headsails!" and we're off for our final full day of sailing. We head westward, back towards Rockland. Sailing off the anchor powered by wind alone. No sound of an engine, no smell of diesel fumes, just the water lapping on the hull. With a brisk wind, we sail through the Fox Islands Thoroughfare, a picturesque passageway between the islands of Vinalhaven and North Haven, and then tack out the east side. We turn north and, as the afternoon sea breeze fills our sails, shoot up the coast of North Haven to our final stop for the trip, Pulpit Harbor. Records of the osprey nest that stands sentry at the entrance of Pulpit Harbor go back over 200 years. It's a real treat to sit at anchor and watch these majestic birds fish for their dinners. It's been an exciting week!

Saturday

Saturday morning we raise anchor early and head back home. Last minute group photos are taken, addresses exchanged, and a brunch spread is served to tide everyone over on their way out of town. We tie up in Rockland amid relaxed, revitalized smiles, and see everyone ashore with hugs and goodbyes.

From the Sea

A mercurial friend, the sea. One day calm and inviting, the next strident and willful. Those that make their trade on the water learn to bend to the will of nature and to the whim of the ocean. The call of the sea is strong and evocative, lingering in the blood long after a perfect day of easy, sweet breeze to push the schooner along in adventure and joy.

Red Clam Sauce with Fusilli

Serves 4 to 6

2 tablespoons unsalted butter
2 cups diced onion; about 1 large onion
2 tablespoons minced garlic; about 6 cloves
1/4 teaspoon kosher salt
several grinds fresh black pepper
1 cup white wine
2 (14-ounce) cans diced tomatoes
1 (6-ounce) can tomato paste
1 (8-ounce) bottle clam juice
8 ounces fresh or dried fusilli
1 (10-ounce) can chopped clams
1/4 cup (1/2 stick) salted butter
1 ounce grated Parmesan cheese; about 1/2 cup lightly packed for garnish
minced fresh Italian parsley for garnish

Melt the butter in a medium stockpot over medium-high heat. Add the onion, garlic, salt, and pepper and sauté for 7 to 10 minutes or until translucent. Add the wine, tomatoes, tomato paste, and clam juice, bring to a boil, reduce heat to low, and simmer for 45 minutes. Meanwhile, bring a large pot of salted water to a boil. Add the pasta and cook until al dente according to the package instructions. When the pasta is almost done, add the clams to the sauce, and cook for 2 minutes or until they are just heated through. Remove from heat and add the butter, stirring until it is incorporated. Serve over pasta and garnish with the cheese and parsley.

Haddock with Herbed Butter, Caramelized Onions, and Tomatoes

Serves 4

Herbed Butter
1 cup (2 sticks) unsalted butter, room temperature
1/2 cup lightly packed fresh basil leaves
1/2 cup lightly packed fresh Italian parsley leaves
1 tablespoon minced shallot; about 1/2 shallot
1 small clove garlic
1/2 teaspoon table salt
several grinds fresh black pepper

Caramelized Onions
1 tablespoon unsalted butter
2 cups sliced onion; about 1 large onion
$\frac{1}{2}$ teaspoon kosher salt
several grinds fresh black pepper
2 tablespoons fresh thyme leaves

2 tablespoons extra virgin olive oil
4 (6 to 8 ounces each) haddock fillets
3 tomatoes, sliced
$\frac{1}{4}$ teaspoon kosher salt
several grinds fresh black pepper

Herbed Butter
Pulse the softened butter, basil, parsley, shallot, garlic, salt, and pepper together in a
food processor. Scrape the butter onto a piece of plastic wrap and form the butter
into a log. Wrap well and chill or freeze.

Caramelized Onions
Heat the butter in a medium skillet over medium-low heat. Add the onion, salt and
pepper, and sauté for 25 to 30 minutes or until the onion is soft and brown. Stir in
the thyme.

Preheat oven to 375°F. Oil a 9- x 13-inch pan. Place the haddock in the pan in a single
layer. Cover the haddock with the caramelized onions and then the sliced tomatoes
and sprinkle with salt and pepper. Bake for 15 to 20 minutes or until the haddock is
still a tiny bit opaque in the middle. It will keep cooking when you remove it from the
oven. Slice the herbed butter into $\frac{1}{4}$-inch medallions and place them on top of the
tomatoes and serve.

Shrimp with Prosciutto and Green Olives on Fettuccine

This is a recipe that came from three years of working with Hans Bucher, my mentor. This was one of his wife's favorite combinations; he served it with pasta or risotto. Sometimes we would wrap the shrimp in prosciutto and grill it while making the sauce with the olives. Serves 4

8 ounces fresh or dried fettuccine
4 tablespoons ($\frac{1}{2}$ stick) unsalted butter (for both the pan and the sauce)
$\frac{2}{3}$ cup green olives, pitted
4 slices prosciutto, diced
2 tablespoons minced garlic; about 6 cloves
2 pounds large shrimp, peeled and deveined
$\frac{2}{3}$ cup white wine
$\frac{1}{4}$ cup fresh lemon juice; about 1 lemon
1 ounce grated Parmesan cheese; about $\frac{1}{2}$ cup lightly packed for garnish
minced fresh Italian parsley for garnish

Bring a large pot of salted water to a boil. Add the pasta and cook until al dente according to the package instructions. Meanwhile, melt the butter in a large sauté pan over medium-high heat. Add the olives and prosciutto and sauté for 1 minute. Add the garlic and sauté for 30 seconds. Add the shrimp and sauté until it is nearly cooked through, about 2 minutes (depending on the size). Add the white wine and lemon juice and continue to cook for 30 seconds. Remove the pan from the heat and gently stir in butter until it's all incorporated. Spoon the shrimp over the pasta and garnish with the cheese and parsley.

Lemon Lobster with Sun-Dried Tomatoes

This recipe was a summer favorite at Jessica's Restaurant when I was sous chef under Chef Hans Bucher. It's important to have all the ingredients ready and on hand before you start. Don't begin sautéing until the pasta is in the water and you've given it a good stir. Also, if you'd like to double the recipe to serve 4 people, use 2 pans— the amount of surface heat is important to get the best results. Serves 2

4 ounces fresh or dried fettuccine
2 tablespoons unsalted butter (for the pan and to finish the sauce)
$\frac{1}{4}$ cup sun-dried tomatoes in oil, oil drained, chopped
2 teaspoons minced shallots; about $\frac{1}{2}$ shallot
8 ounces cooked lobster meat; about 2 (1 pound each) lobsters, claws left
    whole and tails cut into $\frac{1}{4}$-inch slices

^{1}/$_4$ teaspoon kosher salt
several grinds fresh black pepper
^{1}/$_3$ cup white wine
2 tablespoons fresh lemon juice; about ^{1}/$_2$ lemon
1 ounce grated Parmesan cheese; about ^{1}/$_2$ cup lightly packed for garnish
minced fresh Italian parsley for garnish

Bring a large pot of salted water to a boil. Add the pasta and cook until al dente
according to the package instructions. Meanwhile, melt 1 tablespoon of butter in
a large sauté pan over medium-high heat. Add the sun-dried tomatoes; sauté for
1 minute, then add the shallots and sauté for 30 seconds to 1 minute. Add the lobster
meat, salt, and pepper and sauté for 1 minute. Add the white wine and lemon juice;
cook for another 30 seconds; and remove from heat. Gently stir in the other tablespoon of butter until it's completely incorporated. Serve over pasta and garnish with
the cheese and parsley.

Salmon with Tri-Pepper Salsa

This is a great one. Everyone loves it — even folks who normally don't like salmon. A note about the julienned peppers for the salsa: the strips shouldn't be too long; if they are, cut them in half cross-wise. This is mostly a practical thing. If they are too long, you end up sticking them in your nose when you try to eat them. Serves 4

Salsa
1/2 cup julienned red bell pepper; about 1/2 pepper
1/2 cup julienned green bell pepper; about 1/2 pepper
1/2 cup julienned yellow bell pepper; about 1/2 pepper
1 cup thinly sliced red onion; about 1/2 onion
3 tablespoons extra virgin olive oil
3 tablespoons fresh lime juice; about 1 1/2 limes
2 tablespoons minced fresh dill
1/2 teaspoon kosher salt
several grinds fresh black pepper

Salmon
4 (6 to 8 ounces each) skinless salmon fillets
1/4 cup fresh lemon juice; about 1 lemon
1/4 cup extra virgin olive oil
1/4 cup white wine
1 teaspoon kosher salt
several grinds fresh black pepper

Salsa
Toss the peppers and onion with the olive oil, lime juice, and dill in a small bowl. Add salt and pepper to taste. Let the salsa sit at room temperature for an hour (two at the most — you don't want it to get soggy). Check the seasoning again just before you serve. I almost always add a little bit more salt.

Salmon
Preheat oven to 375°F. Place the salmon in a 9- x 13-inch baking pan, preferably a non-reactive one — enamel or ceramic. Drizzle the lemon juice, olive oil, and white wine over the salmon and season with salt and pepper. Let the salmon sit for 15 minutes, then bake, uncovered, for 15 to 20 minutes. Remove the salmon when it is still somewhat darker pink in the center. It will continue to cook once you take it out of the oven, so take it out before it's quite done. Serve the salsa on top of the salmon.

Pommery Mussels

These mussels are wonderful with some crusty bread to sop up the sauce and a big green salad.
Serves 4

4 tablespoons (¹/₂ stick) unsalted butter
2 tablespoons minced shallots; about 1 shallot
2 tablespoons Pommery mustard
3 pounds clean mussels in the shell, beards removed
1¹/₂ cups white wine
¹/₄ cup fresh lemon juice; about 1 lemon
1 teaspoon kosher salt
several grinds fresh black pepper
2 cups diced, peeled, and seeded tomatoes; about 2 tomatoes

Melt the butter in a medium saucepan over medium-high heat. Add the shallots and sauté for 30 seconds to 1 minute. Add the mustard and sauté briefly. Add the mussels, wine, lemon juice, salt, and pepper and stir with a wooden spoon. Simmer for 5 minutes or until the mussels open. Remove the mussels with tongs as each one opens and transfer to a serving bowl. Discard any unopened mussels. When all of the mussels are removed from the pan, pour the pan sauce on top and garnish with the diced tomatoes. Serve immediately.

Sesame Seared Tuna

Serves 4

4 (6 to 8 ounces each) 1-inch thick tuna steaks
¹/₂ cup soy sauce
1 tablespoon minced garlic; about 3 cloves
1 tablespoon peeled and grated fresh ginger
1 tablespoon fresh lime juice; about ¹/₂ lime
3 tablespoons toasted sesame oil
2 tablespoons extra virgin olive oil
¹/₂ cup sesame seeds

Place the tuna on a platter. Whisk the soy sauce, garlic, ginger, lime juice, and sesame oil in a small bowl. Pour over the tuna and marinate the tuna for 1 hour. Heat a large sauté pan on medium-high heat. Drizzle the olive oil into the pan and then sprinkle the sesame seeds evenly in the pan. Gently place the tuna steaks on top of the sesame seeds and sear for 1 to 4 minutes on each side — 2 minutes for medium rare, 3 minutes for medium. Serve on top of Sautéed Greens (page 52).

Lobster Bake

The highlight of the week for many of our guests is our traditional Maine lobster bake— a feature on all our trips. It's an all-you-can-eat feast. After anchoring near an undisturbed island in the early afternoon, the yawl boat ferries us ashore, and we hop across granite rocks to the beach. Everyone wanders off in different directions— exploring inland, walking the shore, swimming— some even help set up for dinner.

The crew has already rowed ashore and brought everything we need to the island. A fire is lit below the high tide mark, corn is shucked, and various goodies are put out to tide us over until the lobster is ready. Once the fire is really going, the lobster pot— a huge galvanized steel tub— is filled with 2 to 3 inches of salt water and set on the fire to boil. While we wait for the water to come to a boil, several armloads of seaweed are gathered (we're careful to never take more than we need). Once the water is boiling we layer the lobsters and corn in the pot, cover it with a "lid" of seaweed, wait for it to come to a boil, and rotate the pot (for even cooking on the fire). Before the discovery of so many food allergies and disciplines, we used to add mussels, clams, onions, potatoes, and sausage. Now, those are all done separately. When the water comes to a second boil, we'll pull some of the seaweed aside and check to see that the lobsters are red all over. When the lobsters are done, the pot is carried away from the fire, the seaweed is arranged on a flat rock, and everything is placed onto the seaweed bed, ready to eat.

Once everyone has had their fill of lobster (Seven lobsters eaten by one person, a 15 year old Girl Scout no less, is still the record. No cheating either, she ate all the meat from the legs too.), dessert is laid out. There's always a lively discussion over how to make the best S'more, and the proper way to roast a marshmallow. We now have all sorts of additions to the traditional S'more like: peanut butter, bananas, strawberries, and campfire waffle cones.

With tongue in cheek, place the Hershey bar on top of one of the halves of graham cracker and place it on a rock near the fire so the chocolate can get warm. Place two marshmallows on a metal roasting stick (not driftwood) and patiently turn it over the hot coals until it becomes brown— the impatient folks wind up with a burnt marshmallow. Some poor souls actually like them this way. Go figure. Slide the marshmallows on top of the chocolate and complete the sandwich with the second graham cracker.

From the Farm

Without the entertainments of modern life that can sometimes separate us from our neighbors, we find ourselves engaging each other on board in the way our ancestors did - with our voices and with instruments like the guitar or penny whistle. The acoustics of sound on the water seems to add a purity to the notes and is an enchanting way to end our day.

Black Forest Pork Stew

Serves 4 to 6

1$\frac{1}{2}$ pounds pork stew meat, cut into $\frac{3}{4}$-inch pieces
$\frac{1}{4}$ cup all-purpose flour
1$\frac{1}{2}$ teaspoons kosher salt (for both the pork and the vegetables)
several grinds fresh black pepper
1 teaspoon paprika
2 tablespoons extra virgin olive oil
2 slices bacon, diced
2 cups diced onion; about 1 large onion
2 cups peeled and diced carrots; about 2 carrots
1 cup diced celery; about 1 stalk
1 tablespoon minced garlic; about 3 cloves
1 (6-ounce) can tomato paste
1 cup white wine
2 cups beef broth
1 pound bratwurst sausage, cut into 1-inch pieces
1$\frac{1}{2}$ tablespoons fresh minced marjoram
6 ounces button mushrooms, quartered; about 2 cups

Toss the pork, flour, salt, pepper, and paprika together in a large bowl to coat the meat. Heat the olive oil in a stockpot over medium-high heat. Add the pork to the pot and cook until browned. Add the bacon and cook for 5 minutes or until the bacon is done. Add the onion, carrots, celery, and garlic and cook for another 10 to 15 minutes until the onion is translucent. Add the tomato paste, white wine, broth, and bratwurst. Reduce heat and simmer, covered, for 2 hours or until the meat is tender. Add the marjoram and mushrooms and cook for another 10 minutes. Serve alone or over spätzle, egg noodles, or mashed potatoes.

Chicken Paprika

If you plan to freeze or refrigerate this dish to serve later, reserve the sour cream. When you reheat, add the sour cream just before serving. Serves 4 to 6

2 tablespoons olive oil
2 pounds boneless, skinless chicken breasts or thighs, cut into 1-inch pieces
1 teaspoon kosher salt
several grinds fresh black pepper
2 cups diced onion; about 1 large onion

1 cup diced green bell pepper; about 1 pepper
1 tablespoon minced garlic; about 3 cloves
1½ tablespoons paprika
¼ cup tomato paste
½ cup red wine
2 (14-ounce) cans diced tomatoes
several dashes of Worcestershire sauce
6 ounces button mushrooms, sliced; about 2 cups
½ cup sour cream

Heat the oil in a large, wide stockpot over medium-high heat. Add the chicken, salt, and pepper in and sauté until browned on all sides. Add the onion, peppers, garlic, and paprika and sauté for another 10 minutes or until the onion is translucent. Add the tomato paste and stir well for about a minute. Add the wine, tomatoes, and Worcestershire. Reduce heat to low cover, and simmer for 45 minutes or until the chicken is tender. Add the mushrooms and cook another 5 minutes. Stir in the sour cream and serve with noodles, potatoes, or polenta.

Rosemary and Dijon Riggin Rib Roast with Horseradish Cream

No rib roast would be complete without Yorkshire pudding (page 82). Serves 6 to 8

1 (6- to 8-pound) standing bone-in beef rib roast
1 teaspoon kosher salt
several grinds fresh black pepper
1 teaspoon paprika
1 tablespoon Dijon mustard
1 tablespoon minced garlic; about 3 cloves
1 tablespoon chopped fresh rosemary

Preheat oven to 425°F. Place the roast in a roasting pan fat side up and rub with salt, pepper, and paprika. Transfer the roast to the oven, reduce heat to 325°F, and cook for 1 to 1½ hours. Rub the roast with the remaining ingredients; return it to the oven and continue to roast to the desired temperature until the internal temperature of the meat reads 120°F for rare, 125°F for medium-rare, 130°F for medium, and 135°F for well done. Remove the roast from the oven and let it rest 10 minutes before slicing. While the roast is resting, make the Horseradish Cream (see below).

Horseradish Cream

The amount of salt needed will vary depending on whether you use bottled or fresh horseradish. Makes 1½ cups

3 tablespoons bottled or freshly grated horseradish
table salt as needed
several grinds fresh black pepper
2 tablespoons fresh lemon juice; about ½ lemon
1 cup heavy cream, whipped to soft peaks

Mix all the ingredients except the whipped cream together. Gently fold in the whipped cream and serve.

New England Boiled Dinner with Mustard Sauce

This is a classic that never seems to go out of favor. Of course, any leftover meat and veggies can be cut up and cooked into a hash with poached eggs and a fresh salsa. Serves 8

1 (6 pound) corned beef brisket
1 pound carrots, peeled and cut into 1¹/₂-inch chunks
12 to 16 small red-skinned potatoes, skin on
12 to 16 small white onions, peeled
1 large turnip, peeled and cut into 1¹/₂-inch chunks
1 large head of cabbage, cored and cut into eight wedges

Place the corned beef in a large stew pot and cover with water. Cover, bring to a boil, reduce heat, and simmer for 2 to 3 hours or until tender when pierced with a fork. Remove the meat from the pot, reserving the liquid. Place the potatoes and turnip in the pot and boil for 15 minutes. Add the carrots and onions and boil for 10 more minutes. Add the cabbage and boil for another 5 minutes. Strain all the vegetables into a colander. Slice the beef diagonally against the grain. Arrange the meat and vegetables on a platter and serve with Mustard Sauce (see below) and Irish Soda Bread (page 156).

Mustard Sauce

Makes about 1 cup

2 tablespoons dry mustard
1 teaspoon all-purpose flour
¹/₂ teaspoon table salt
1 can evaporated milk
¹/₄ cup sugar
1 large egg yolk
¹/₂ cup heated apple cider vinegar

Mix together the mustard, flour, and salt. Add ¹/₃ cup of evaporated milk and whisk until there are no lumps. Put the sugar and the rest of the evaporated milk in a double boiler over medium heat. Whisk in the mustard mixture, then whisk in the eggs. Heat, whisking frequently, until the mixture thickens. Remove the mixture from the heat and whisk in the heated vinegar. Leave it in the double boiler until you're ready to serve to keep warm. Transfer to a pitcher and serve.

Mom's Spaghetti with Meatballs

This is the meal that as kids we would ask for more than any other. It was our favorite birthday dinner for many years. Mom would make the meatballs big, so we had a rule that we could only have two meatballs per person, thankfully, in our household, a third is allowed. If there are any leftovers, something not likely in our house, the sauce and meatballs are easily frozen, either together or separately. Serves 4 to 6

Sauce
2 tablespoons extra virgin olive oil
1½ cups diced onion; about 1 medium onion
¾ teaspoon kosher salt
1 teaspoon sugar
¼ teaspoon dried oregano
¼ teaspoon dried basil
¼ teaspoon crushed red pepper
1 tablespoons dried parsley flakes
1 (6-ounce) can tomato paste
1 (28-ounce) can pureed tomatoes
1 (16-ounce) can crushed or diced tomatoes

Meatballs
1½ pounds ground beef
¾ cup breadcrumbs
¾ teaspoon kosher salt
½ teaspoon dried oregano
1½ teaspoons minced garlic; about 2 cloves
several grinds fresh black pepper
1 large egg

8 ounces fresh or dried spaghetti

Sauce
Heat the oil in a large stockpot over medium-high heat. Add the onion and salt and sauté for 7 to 10 minutes or until the onion is translucent. Add the sugar, herbs, and tomato paste and sauté for another 5 minutes, stirring often. Add the rest of the ingredients and bring to a boil. Reduce heat to low and simmer for 2 hours, stirring occasionally. While the sauce is simmering make the meatballs.

Meatballs
Preheat oven to 350°F. Mix the meatball ingredients together in a medium-sized bowl with your hands. Form about sixteen 2-inch meatballs with either a scoop or your hands and place the meatballs on a rimmed baking sheet. Bake for 30 minutes or until cooked through. Drain off the fat and transfer the meatballs into the sauce. Simmer for another 30 minutes.

Bring a large pot of salted water to a boil. Add the pasta and cook until al dente according to the package instructions.

Bolognese Sauce

When I make this sauce in the middle of the summer and the herb garden is bursting at the seams, I use fresh herbs in place of the dried and add them at the end. In the middle of winter, dried herbs work well, but they should go in at the beginning to allow their flavor to develop. Serves 4 to 6

1 tablespoon extra virgin olive oil
$^1/_2$ pound ground beef
1 teaspoon kosher salt
several grinds fresh black pepper
1 cup diced onion; about 1 medium onion
$^1/_2$ cup diced green bell pepper; about $^1/_2$ pepper
2 tablespoons minced garlic; about 6 cloves
1 tablespoon dried basil
1 tablespoon dried oregano
1 teaspoon dried thyme
1 teaspoon dried marjoram
2 (28-ounce) cans diced tomatoes
2 cups red wine
4 ounces button mushrooms, quartered; about $1^1/_2$ cups
8 ounces fresh or dried spaghetti

Heat the olive oil in a large pot over medium heat. Brown the ground beef with the salt and pepper. Add the onion, pepper, garlic, and herbs, and sauté until translucent. Add the tomatoes and red wine and bring to a boil. Reduce heat to low and simmer, covered, for 2 hours stirring occasionally. Add the mushrooms at the end and cook for another 10 minutes. To serve, bring a large pot of salted water to a boil. Add the pasta and cook until al dente according to the package instructions.

Sage, Rosemary, and Salt-Rubbed Roast Pork Loin with Cranberry Port Sauce

The rub for this recipe creates such a moist roast with tons of flavor. Begin the day before to give the rub time to really sink into the roast. Serves 4 to 6

$^3/_4$ cup chopped fresh parsley
$^3/_4$ cup chopped fresh sage
3 tablespoons chopped fresh rosemary
2 teaspoons kosher salt
several grinds fresh black pepper
$^1/_4$ cup extra virgin olive oil
1 (3 pound) boneless pork loin roast

Combine all the ingredients except the pork in a small bowl. Rub the pork loin all over with the herb mixture, cover, and refrigerate overnight.

Preheat oven to 375°F. Place the pork in a roasting pan and roast for 1 hour or until the internal temperature of the meat reaches 145°F for medium and 150°F for medium well. Remove the pork from the oven and let it rest, covered, for 10 minutes. Slice and serve with the Cranberry Port Sauce (see below).

Cranberry Port Sauce

Makes about 2 cups

8 ounces fresh cranberries; about 2 cups
6 tablespoons port
6 tablespoons sugar
2 tablespoons orange zest; about $^1/_2$ orange
2 tablespoons fresh orange juice
$^1/_8$-inch thick slice fresh ginger
1 tablespoon red currant jelly

Combine the cranberries, port, sugar, orange juice, orange zest, and ginger in a small non-reactive saucepan. Bring the mixture to a boil over medium-high heat, stirring to dissolve the sugar. Reduce heat to low and simmer for 12 to 15 minutes, stirring frequently, until the cranberries have popped and the sauce is slightly thickened. Discard the ginger slice, stir in the jelly, and set aside to cool slightly. Serve with Roast Pork Loin (see above).

Braised Lamb Shanks with Thyme, Cinnamon, and Fennel

Serves 4

4 (³/₄ to 1 pound each) lamb shanks
1 teaspoon kosher salt
several grinds fresh black pepper
2 tablespoons canola oil
2 cups diced onion; about 1 large onion
2 cups peeled and diced carrots; about 2 carrots
2 cups peeled and diced parsnips; about 2 parsnips
4 fresh thyme sprigs
2 whole garlic heads; unpeeled, cut in half horizontally
1 cup dry red wine
5 cups chicken broth
1 large orange, peeled, quartered and pith cut away
2 whole cinnamon sticks
1 teaspoon fennel seeds, crushed

Preheat oven to 375°F. Season the lamb with salt and pepper. Heat the oil in a large, oven-proof pot over high heat. Add the lamb and cook until brown on all sides, about 10 minutes. Transfer the lamb to a platter. Add the onion, carrots, parsnips, thyme, and garlic to the pot and sauté for 7 to 10 minutes or until the vegetables soften and begin to brown. Add the wine and bring to a boil for about 4 minutes or until the liquid is reduced almost to a glaze. Return the lamb shanks to the pot, arranging them in a single layer. Add the broth, orange, cinnamon sticks, and fennel seeds and bring to a boil. Place the pot in the oven and cook for 2 hours, uncovered, or until the lamb is tender and almost falling off the bone. Turn and baste often. Transfer the lamb to a platter again and tent with aluminum foil to keep warm. Strain the braising liquid into a bowl and spoon off the fat. Return the liquid to the pot. Simmer for 15 minutes or until the sauce is thick enough to coat the back of a spoon. Return the lamb to the pot; cover and warm over medium-low heat for 5 minutes or until the lamb is completely reheated and serve.

Zucchini and Genoa Salami Deep Dish Pizza

Serves 8 to 12

2 tablespoons extra virgin olive oil (plus extra for the pan and crust)
4 cups diced zucchini; about 2 zucchini
4 cups diced summer squash; about 2 squash
1/2 teaspoon kosher salt
several grinds fresh black pepper
1 Crusty Peasant Bread dough recipe (page 140) or 2 pounds pre-made
    dough
2 ounces grated Parmesan cheese; about 1 cup lightly packed
1 pound Genoa salami, cut in medium-thick slices
4 ounces grated mozzarella cheese; about 1 cup lightly packed
2 cups whole milk ricotta cheese
dried basil and oregano to sprinkle on the crust

Oil a 9- x 13-inch baking pan. Heat the olive oil in a large sauté pan over medium-high heat. Add the zucchini, summer squash, salt, and pepper and sauté for 7 to 10 minutes or until tender. Divide the dough roughly in half, making one part slightly larger than the other. Either roll or use your hands to stretch the larger piece until it's big enough to overlap over the sides of the baking pan by about 1-inch. Spread half of the Parmesan cheese evenly over the dough. Layer half of the salami, mozzarella, ricotta, zucchini, and summer squash. When you transfer the squash to the pizza, use a slotted spoon to drain the excess liquid. Repeat with the remaining half. Roll the remaining dough out enough to overlap the top of the pan. Transfer the dough and then pinch the two layers of dough together neatly at the edges. Brush the crust with the olive oil and sprinkle with the herbs. Preheat oven to 350°F. Let the pizza rest and rise for 30 minutes. Bake for 1 hour or until golden brown. Cool 15 minutes before cutting and serving.

"Lamb"sagna

Serves 6 to 8

1/4 cup extra virgin olive oil (for both the pan and the zucchini)
1 pound ground lamb
3/4 teaspoon kosher salt (for both the lamb and the zucchini)
several grinds fresh black pepper
2 cups diced onion; about 1 large onion
2 tablespoons minced garlic; about 6 cloves
2 tablespoons minced fresh basil

2 tablespoons all-purpose flour
1 cup whole milk
4 zucchini and/or summer squash, sliced lengthwise ¼-inch thick
4 large tomatoes, sliced ¼-inch thick
1½ cups breadcrumbs
2 ounces crumbled feta cheese; about 1 cup

Preheat oven to 350°F. Heat 2 tablespoons of oil in a medium saucepan over medium-high heat. Add the lamb, ½ teaspoon salt, and pepper. Add the onion, garlic, and basil and sauté for 7 to 10 minutes or until the onion is translucent. Sprinkle with the flour and combine well. Add the milk and bring it to a simmer. Remove from heat. Heat another 2 tablespoons of olive oil in a separate skillet. Add the sliced zucchini and/or summer squash, another ¼ teaspoon salt, and pepper and sauté in a single layer until they begin to brown on both sides. Repeat as needed to cook the squash. Layer half of the squash, lamb, and tomatoes in a 9- x 13-inch baking pan. Repeat with the remaining squash, lamb, and tomatoes. Sprinkle with breadcrumbs and feta cheese. Bake for 45 minutes or until the cheese is brown and bubbling. Remove from oven and cool 10 minutes before serving.

Riggin Ham with Roasted Onions and Red Pepper Glaze

Woodstoves are perfect for cooking large cuts of meat. Ham, especially when locally cured, can be really special when done in a woodstove. When buying a ham at the grocery store, look for hams without the labels "ham, water added" or "ham and water product." Red Pepper Jam is just one of many ideas for glazing ham— use homemade jams, mustard, dried fruit, and/or brown sugar to create something out of the ordinary. Serves 12 to 14

1 (7- to 10-pound) cured ham
1 cup Red Pepper Jam (page 34)
8 large onions, peeled and cut into eighths

Preheat oven to 350°F. Place the ham in a roasting pan and roast for 1 hour. Add the onions and roast for another hour or until the internal temperature of the meat reads 120°F. Remove the ham from the oven. If the onions are soft and golden, remove them and set aside. If not, continue to roast them with the ham. Spread half of the red pepper jelly liberally over the ham. Return the ham to the oven, basting frequently for about 20 minutes or until the jelly is golden brown. Allow the ham to rest for 15 minutes before slicing. Combine the pan juices with the other half of the jelly and serve with the ham and roasted onions.

Pork Tenderloin with Creamy Caper Sauce

This sauce is also wonderful with chicken or salmon. Serves 4

2 (1 pound each) pork tenderloins
several grinds fresh black pepper
1 teaspoon kosher salt (plus extra for the onion)
1 teaspoon paprika
2 tablespoons extra virgin olive oil
2 cups diced onion; about 1 large onion
4 teaspoons minced garlic; about 4 cloves
2 cups peeled, seeded and chopped diced tomato; about 2 tomatoes
2 teaspoons fresh minced basil
2 teaspoons fresh minced tarragon
½ cup white wine
3 to 4 tablespoons chicken broth or water
1 cup heavy cream
¼ cup capers

Rub the tenderloins with the salt, pepper, and paprika. Heat the oil in a large oven-proof sauté pan over medium-high heat. Add the tenderloins and sear until well-browned on all sides. Reduce heat to medium and add the onion, garlic, and salt. Sauté for 7 to 10 minutes or until the onion is translucent. Turn the tenderloins occasionally while the onion is cooking. Add the tomatoes and herbs and cook for another minute. Add the wine, broth, and heavy cream and bring to a simmer. Continue simmering for about 10 minutes or until the pork reaches an internal temperature of 145°F for medium and 150°F for medium well. Transfer the tenderloins to a cutting board to rest. Transfer the pan sauce to a blender and puree until smooth. Add the capers. Cut the tenderloins on an angle into ¼- to ½-inch slices and serve with the sauce.

Chicken and Winter Veggie Stew

Serves 4 to 6

2 tablespoons unsalted butter
1 pound boneless, skinless chicken breasts or thighs, cut into 1-inch pieces
1½ cups chopped onion; about 1 medium onion
1½ cups chopped celery; about 2 stalks
3 cups peeled and sliced (½-inch thick) carrots; about 3 carrots
2 cups peeled and sliced (½-inch thick) parsnips; about 2 parsnips

1 tablespoon minced fresh tarragon
1 tablespoon minced fresh thyme
1 teaspoon kosher salt
several grinds freshly ground black pepper
3 tablespoons all-purpose flour
½ cup white wine
4 to 6 cups chicken broth
1 cup frozen peas
4 ounces button mushrooms, sliced ¼-inch thick; about 2 cups

Heat the oil in a large pot over medium-high heat. Brown the chicken on all sides and set aside. In the same pan, add the onion, carrots, parsnips, paprika, garlic, herbs, salt, and pepper and sauté for 10 minutes or until the onion is translucent. Sprinkle the flour into the pan and stir well. Add the wine, chicken broth, and the reserved chicken and bring to a boil. Reduce heat to low and simmer for 45 minutes or until the chicken is tender. Ten minutes before serving, add the peas and the mushrooms. Serve with Baking Powder Biscuits (page 152) or Annie's Mashed Potatoes (page 80).

Chicken Curry

On board ships, sailors would use spices acquired in the Caribbean islands to flavor their food. Spices added flavor, but were also used for practical reasons — to cover the smell of less than fresh meat. With refrigeration that's certainly not a problem these days, but it's an interesting bit of history. The condiments we serve with the curry make a very festive presentation; the table overflows with bowls and platters. Serves 4 to 6

2 tablespoons canola oil
2 pounds boneless, skinless chicken thighs cut into 1-inch pieces
2 cups diced onion; about 1 large onion
1 cup diced green bell pepper; about 1 pepper
$\frac{1}{2}$ jalapeño pepper, seeded and minced (optional)
2 teaspoons minced garlic; about 2 cloves
1 tablespoon grated fresh ginger
2 tablespoons curry powder
1 teaspoon ground cumin
1 teaspoon kosher salt
1 (14-ounce) can diced tomatoes
1 (13.5 ounce) can coconut milk
2 tablespoons fresh lime juice; about 1 lime

Heat the oil in a large, wide stockpot over medium-high heat. Place the chicken in the pot and cook until browned on all sides. Add the onion, peppers, garlic, ginger, spices, and salt and cook for another 10 minutes or until the onion is translucent. Add the tomatoes, coconut milk, and lime. Reduce heat to low and simmer for 45 minutes or until chicken is tender. Serve over couscous or rice; with any of the condiments (page 117); and/or the Cantaloupe Raita (see below).

Cantaloupe Raita

Raita, typically yogurt and cucumbers, is used to "cool down" the spiciness of the curry. Cantaloupe is an interesting twist. Makes 3 cups

1 cup diced cantaloupe
2 cups plain yogurt
1 tablespoon minced fresh cilantro
$\frac{1}{4}$ teaspoon table salt
several grinds fresh black pepper

Mix everything together. Serve immediately.

Condiments: diced bananas, apples, peanuts, hardboiled eggs, bell peppers, onions, shredded coconut, lime wedges, raisins

Curried Lamb and Lentil Stew

Serves 4 to 6

2 tablespoons extra virgin olive oil
2 pounds lamb stew meat, cut into $^3/_4$-inch pieces
1 teaspoon kosher salt
several grinds fresh black pepper
2 cups diced onion; about 1 large onion
2 cups peeled and diced carrots; about 2 carrots
2 tablespoons minced garlic; about 6 cloves
1 tablespoon grated fresh ginger
2 tablespoons curry powder
1 cup red wine
3 cups beef broth
3 cups peeled and diced yellow-fleshed potatoes, cut into $^1/_2$-inch cubes;
    about 2 medium potatoes
1 cup du Puy or French lentils
crumbled feta cheese for garnish
raisins for garnish
roasted sunflower seeds for garnish

Heat the olive oil in a large pot over medium-high heat. Add the lamb, salt, and pepper and sauté for 10 minutes or until browned on all sides. Add the onion, carrots, garlic, ginger, and curry and sauté for 7 to 10 minutes or until the onion is translucent. Add the red wine and beef broth. Cover, reduce heat, and simmer for 1 hour or until the meat is nearly tender. Add the potatoes and lentils and more broth if needed and continue to simmer for another 20 to 25 minutes until the potatoes and lentils are cooked. Serve over a bed of spinach, jasmine rice, or polenta.

Rosemary Chicken and Dumplings

Serves 4 to 6

Chicken
2 tablespoons olive oil
1 (4½ pound) whole chicken, cut into 8 pieces
¼ cup all-purpose flour
1 teaspoon kosher salt
several grinds fresh black pepper
1 teaspoon paprika
2 cups diced onion; about 1 large onion
2 cups peeled and diced carrots; about 2 carrots
2 cups diced celery; about 3 stalks
1 tablespoon minced garlic; about 3 cloves
1 tablespoon minced fresh Italian parsley
2 tablespoons minced fresh thyme
3 tablespoons minced fresh rosemary
1 cup white wine
2 cups chicken broth

Dumplings
2 cups all-purpose flour
1 tablespoon baking powder
1 teaspoon table salt
¼ cup butter
2 tablespoons minced fresh parsley
¾ cup whole milk

Chicken
Heat the oil in a large, wide stockpot over medium-high heat. Toss the chicken, flour, salt, pepper and paprika together until the chicken is well coated. Place the chicken in the heated pot and cook until browned on all sides. Remove the chicken to a platter and set aside. Add the onion, carrots, celery, garlic, and herbs to the pot and sauté for another 7 to 10 minutes until the vegetables are translucent. Return the chicken to the pot and add the white wine and broth. Bring to a boil, reduce heat to low, and simmer, covered, for 1 hour until the chicken is tender.

Dumplings

Sift the dry ingredients into a medium bowl. Use a pastry cutter to cut the butter into the flour until it resembles a fine meal. Make a well in the center and stir in the parsley and milk until the dough comes together in a ball. Drop 1-inch balls of dough on top of the simmering chicken. Cover and cook an additional 10 minutes. NO PEEKING! The dumplings are done when the dough is cooked through in the center.

Roasted 5-Herb Chicken

If you are in a hurry, butterfly or spatchcock the chicken by cutting the chicken through the breastbone and laying it flat on a baking sheet. It will reduce the cooking time by about 45 minutes. The herbs in the classic blend, Herbs de Provence, are not always the same. The ones I like to use are thyme, rosemary, basil, savory, and lavender buds. Others I've seen added are fennel, marjoram, and mints. Most grocery stores carry a pre-mixed version, so it's not necessary to buy each herb individually.
Serves 4 to 6

1 (4$\frac{1}{2}$ pound) whole chicken
2 tablespoons extra virgin olive oil
2 tablespoons Herbs de Provence
1 teaspoon paprika
1 teaspoon kosher salt
several grinds fresh black pepper
2 tablespoons Dijon mustard

Preheat oven to 400°F. Rub the chicken outside and inside with the oil, herbs, paprika, salt, and pepper. Bake for 1$\frac{1}{2}$ hours or until the legs feel loose in the joint. Transfer the chicken to a serving platter. Whisk the mustard into the pan to make a pan sauce, adding a little water if needed to loosen the sticky bits on the bottom of the pan. Serve with mashed potatoes.

Variation

Lemon Garlic Chicken: Follow the instructions above and stuff the chicken with one whole lemon cut in half and two heads of garlic. If butterflied, place the chicken on top of the lemon and garlic, then roast.

Cornish Game Hens with Smoked Shrimp and Brandy Stuffing

Serves 4

Stuffing
2 tablespoons unsalted butter
$\frac{1}{2}$ cup minced onion; about 1 small onion
$\frac{1}{2}$ cup minced celery; about 1 stalk
1 tablespoon minced shallot; about $\frac{1}{2}$ shallot
$\frac{1}{4}$ teaspoon kosher salt
4 cups day old French bread, cut into $\frac{1}{2}$-inch pieces
1 tablespoon brandy
$\frac{1}{2}$ cup chicken broth
$\frac{3}{4}$ cup smoked Ducktrap shrimp (or smoked oysters)

Hens
4 (1$\frac{1}{2}$ pounds each) Cornish game hens
$\frac{1}{4}$ cup extra virgin olive oil
1 teaspoon kosher salt
several grinds fresh black pepper
1 teaspoon paprika

Stuffing
Preheat oven to 375°F. Heat the butter in a medium skillet over medium heat. Add the onion, celery, shallots, and salt and sauté for 7 minutes or until the vegetables are translucent. Add the mixture to the remaining stuffing ingredients in a medium bowl and gently toss until everything is mixed.

Hens
Rub the outside and inside of the hens with the oil, salt, pepper, and paprika. Stuff the hens and transfer to a baking pan. Roast for 1 hour or until the legs feel loose in the joints and an internal thermometer reads 170°F when inserted into the thigh. Serve immediately.

Puff Pastry Pork and Herb Pot Pie

Serves 4

2 tablespoons olive oil
1 pound pork stew meat, cut into ¾-inch pieces
1 cup chopped fennel; about ½ fennel bulb
2 cups diced onion; about 1 large onion
2 cups peeled and diced carrots; about 2 carrots
2 tablespoons chopped fresh sage
2 tablespoons minced fresh rosemary
2 tablespoons minced garlic; about 6 cloves
1 teaspoon kosher salt
several grinds fresh black pepper
¼ cup all-purpose flour
2 tablespoons tomato paste
3 cups beef broth
1 frozen puff pastry sheet
1 large egg

Set the puff pastry out to defrost slightly. Preheat oven to 350°F. Roll the puff pastry to slightly larger than 10-inches. Spoon the pork into a 10-inch round oven-proof ceramic dish. Press the edges to neatly seal the pastry to the pan. Whisk the egg in a small bowl and brush over the top of the pastry. Bake for 30 minutes or until the surface is golden brown.

Variation
Divide the stew evenly between 4 oven-proof bowls and top with puff pastry. Reduce baking time to 20 to 25 minutes.

Sautéed Beef Tenderloin Filets with Port and Mushroom Sauce

Serves 4

4 (6 to 8 ounces each) 1- to 1½-inch thick beef tenderloin filets
3 tablespoons extra virgin olive oil
¼ teaspoon kosher salt
several grinds fresh black pepper
1 tablespoon unsalted butter
1 tablespoon minced shallots; about ½ shallot
8 ounces button mushrooms, sliced; about 3 cups
3 tablespoons port
½ teaspoon Worcestershire sauce
3 tablespoons unsalted butter

Preheat the oven to 350°F. Rub the filets with the oil, salt, and pepper. Heat a large oven-proof skillet over medium-high heat. Add the tenderloin and sear on both sides until well-browned about 6 to 7 minutes total. Transfer the skillet to the oven and cook for another 5 to 6 minutes or until an internal-read thermometer registers the desired temperature, 125°F for medium-rare. Remove the tenderloins and set them aside on a platter tented with foil.

Return the skillet to the stove top and heat over medium heat. Add the butter and shallots. Sauté for 30 seconds to 1 minute. Add the mushrooms and sauté them until they are nearly cooked through. Whisk in the port and Worcestershire and bring to a simmer for 2 minutes. Remove the pan from the heat and gently whisk in the butter. Serve with the filets.

Variations
Sherry, Pepper, and Tomato: Replace the port with sherry. Omit the mushrooms. Add 2 cups diced tomatoes and extra freshly ground black pepper.
Caramelized Onion and Lemon: Replace the port with white wine. Add the onions with the mushrooms and add 2 tablespoons fresh lemon juice.
Fresh Herbs and Olive: Omit the mushrooms. Add ¼ cup fresh minced herbs and 1 cup minced Kalamata olives.

Grilled Chicken with Passion Fruit Sauce

This recipe is so quick that it's been the saving grace on more than one occasion. Originally created in the Caribbean during our years on yachts, it's lovely on a summer day or a winter one when a little taste of the tropics soothes a snow-crusted soul. Serves 4

2 whole boneless chicken breasts, split
$1/4$ cup extra virgin olive oil
$1/2$ teaspoon kosher salt
several grinds fresh black pepper
$1/4$ cup fresh lime juice; about 2 limes

Combine all of the ingredients in a resealable plastic bag or bowl and marinate the chicken breasts for at least half an hour. Grill over medium-high heat until the chicken is cooked through, turning once on each side to create grill marks. Serve with Passion Fruit Sauce (see below).

Passion Fruit Sauce

Makes 1 cup

4 to 6 passion fruits
1 tablespoon honey
1 tablespoon fresh lime juice; about $1/2$ lime
$1/4$ cup fresh orange juice; about $1/2$ orange

Scoop the insides of the passion fruit into a food processor and add the remaining ingredients. Pulse for 1 minute and then strain into a small bowl. Add additional orange juice to thin the sauce if needed and serve with the chicken.

From the Land

There's something quite instinctive about cooking over a live flame fed with wood. The fire needs constant attention, but not in a fussy way so as to nag, instead as a dance between the one who tends and the one who is tended. Staying present to the stove is a constant - hearing the crackle of new wood, feeling the blast of heat when the oven door is opened, and noticing when the wind changes to require an adjustment at the damper.

Prosciutto, Tomato, and Fontina Strata

This strata is a staple recipe from my family, pulled out for every brunch, shower, or funeral. It's forgiving, flexible, and really, really good. It's perfect for a little bit of this or that which is leftover from a previous meal. Serves 4 to 6

4 cups day old French or Italian bread, cut into ³/₄-inch pieces
6 large eggs
1 tablespoons salted butter, melted
2 cups whole milk
2 tablespoons minced fresh Italian parsley
1 teaspoon dried mustard
2 ounces grated Fontina cheese; about 2 cups lightly packed
1 cup diced tomatoes; about 1 tomato
2 ounces sliced prosciutto, cut in half and then in ¹/₄-inch strips;
    about ¹/₂ cup

Preheat oven to 350°F. Place the bread in the bottom of a 9- x 9-inch pan. Beat the eggs in a large bowl and combine with the rest of the ingredients. Pour over the bread and bake for 20 to 30 minutes. For baking in ramekins, reduce the baking time to 15 to 20 minutes.

For baking ahead and freezing: follow the above directions and cool to room temperature before covering and freezing. Freeze for up to one month. Defrost in the refrigerator overnight and then reheat at 325°F for 20 minutes or until warmed through.

Variations
Corn, Bacon, and Cheddar: Replace the Fontina with cheddar; tomatoes with fresh corn kernels; and prosciutto with cooked and crumbled bacon.
Genoa Salami and Caramelized Onion: Replace prosciutto with salami. Add ¹/₂ cup of caramelized onion.
Smoked Salmon and Dill: Replace the parsley with 1 teaspoons fresh dill and the prosciutto with smoked salmon. Lay the salmon over the bread and then pour the egg and milk mixture over.
Salsa, Chorizo, and Pepper Jack Cheese: Replace Fontina with pepper jack cheese, the tomatoes with ¹/₂ cup salsa, and prosciutto with chorizo.
Ham, Asparagus and Boursin: Replace the Fontina with 1 cup Boursin, prosciutto with ham, and add 1 cup asparagus. Dot the bread with pats of Boursin and then pour the egg and milk mixture over.

Puttanesca

This sauce is delicious served with grilled fish. Alternately, white beans and greens over large crostini make a wonderful base to dress with this sauce. Serves 4 to 6

3 tablespoons olive oil
1 tablespoon minced garlic; about 3 cloves
1 cup Kalamata olives, pitted
2 tablespoons capers
3 anchovies, finely chopped or mashed with the back of a spoon
3 cups peeled and seeded diced tomatoes, or 1 (28-ounce) can
   diced tomatoes
several grinds fresh black pepper
1 ounce grated Parmesan cheese; about ½ cup lightly packed for garnish
minced fresh Italian parsley for garnish

Heat the oil in a sauté pan over medium-high heat. Add garlic and sauté for 30 seconds. Add the olives, capers, and anchovies. Add the tomatoes and pepper and sauté, stirring frequently, about 10 minutes. Serve over hearty greens, polenta, or pasta and garnish with cheese and parsley.

Roasted Mushroom and Artichoke Sauce

Serves 4 to 6

1 pound whole button mushrooms
¼ cup extra virgin olive oil
1½ teaspoon kosher salt (for the mushrooms and the sauce)
several grinds fresh black pepper (for the mushrooms and the sauce)
2 fresh artichokes
¼ cup fresh lemon juice; about 1 lemon
2 tablespoons unsalted butter
2 cups diced onion; about 1 large onion
3 tablespoons minced garlic; about 9 cloves
2 tablespoons all-purpose flour
2 cups vegetable broth (or more)
2 cups peeled and seeded diced tomatoes, or 1 (14-ounce) can
  diced tomatoes
3 tablespoons Marsala wine
2 cups heavy cream
2 teaspoons minced fresh basil
2 teaspoons minced fresh thyme
1 ounce grated Parmesan cheese; about ½ cup lightly packed (plus extra
  for garnish)

Preheat oven to 450°F. Place the mushrooms on a roasting pan, drizzle with olive oil, and sprinkle with salt and pepper. Roast the mushrooms for 15 to 20 minutes or until they begin to slightly brown. Cool and slice the mushrooms. Set aside.

Meanwhile, trim and cut the artichokes into eighths. Take the choke (that's the fuzzy part) out with a spoon. Fill a bowl with water and add the lemon juice and artichokes. Melt the butter in a large pot over medium-high heat. Add the onion, garlic, ½ teaspoon salt, and pepper and reduce heat to medium. Sauté, stirring frequently, for 20 to 30 minutes or until the onion is caramelized. Sprinkle the flour on top of the onion and stir for a minute or so. Add the broth and stir vigorously. Add the tomatoes, Marsala, cream, herbs, and reserved mushrooms and bring to simmer. Add the artichokes and simmer for 20 minutes or until the artichokes are tender. Serve with polenta, pasta, or greens and garnish with the cheese.

Roasted Pine Nut and Eggplant Sauce

Serves 4 to 6

1 large eggplant, peeled and diced
1 teaspoon kosher salt (for both the eggplant and the sauce)
2 tablespoons extra virgin olive oil
2 cups diced onion; about 1 large onion
several grinds fresh black pepper
1 tablespoon minced garlic; about 3 cloves
3 cups peeled and seeded diced tomatoes, or 1 (28-ounce) can
    diced tomatoes
³/₄ cup red wine
2 tablespoons minced fresh basil
¹/₂ cup pine nuts

Place the eggplant in a strainer and lightly sprinkle with ¹/₂ teaspoon salt. Set aside
to drain excess liquid for up to an hour. Heat the olive oil in a large pot over medium
heat and add the onion, ¹/₂ teaspoon salt, and pepper. Sauté for 7 to 10 minutes or
until the onion is translucent. Add the eggplant and garlic and sauté for another
10 minutes or until the eggplant browns. Add the remaining ingredients except the
pine nuts. Simmer for 30 minutes. While the sauce is simmering place the pine nuts
in a small sauté pan and roast them over medium heat for 4 to 5 minutes or until they
are golden brown, stirring often. When you are ready to serve, either stir in the pine
nuts or sprinkle them on top. Serve with polenta, couscous, or pasta.

Roasted garlic is about as versatile as it gets. When we have
"Pasta Night" on board I serve it so that folks can spread it on their
bread, mush it into their sauce, or plunk a few into their salad. I also
use it in egg dishes, soups, stews, sauces, and dressings. Preheat oven
to 400°F. Slice the top off the garlic heads and rub away any loose
skin. Drizzle with olive oil and roast for 35 to 40 minutes or until
tender and golden brown on top.

Tomato, Leek, and Brie Linguini

Serves 4

8 ounces fresh or dried linguini
2 tablespoons unsalted butter
2 teaspoons minced garlic; about 2 cloves
4 cups diced leeks, cut in half lengthwise and thoroughly washed;
    about 2 leeks
1/2 teaspoon kosher salt
several grinds fresh black pepper
4 cups peeled, seeded, and diced tomatoes; about 4 tomatoes
1/3 cup white wine
8 ounces Brie, cut into 1/2-inch cubes

Bring a large pot of salted water to a boil. Add the pasta and cook until al dente according to the package instructions. Meanwhile melt the butter in a sauté pan over medium heat. Add the leeks, salt, and pepper and sauté for 7 to 10 minutes or until tender. Add the garlic and sauté for 30 seconds to 1 minute. Add the tomatoes and wine and bring the sauce to a simmer. Whisk in the Brie a few pieces at a time. When the Brie is melted, toss with the linguini, and serve.

Tomato, Mascarpone, and Kalamata Olive Fettuccine

Serves 4

8 ounces fresh or dried fettuccine
1 tablespoon extra virgin olive oil
1 tablespoon minced garlic; about 3 cloves
2 cups peeled, seeded, and diced plum tomatoes; about 4 to 5 tomatoes
1 1/2 cups Kalamata olives, pitted
8 ounces Mascarpone cheese; about 1 cup
2 tablespoons white wine
1/4 teaspoon kosher salt
several grinds fresh black pepper
2 ounces grated Parmesan cheese; about 1 cup lightly packed
1/4 cup chopped fresh Italian parsley

Bring a large pot of salted water to a boil. Add the pasta and cook until al dente according to the package instructions. Meanwhile heat a sauté pan over medium heat. Add the olive oil and garlic and sauté for about 30 seconds to 1 minute. Add the tomatoes and olives and toss lightly, sautéing for a minute or so. Add the wine, Mascarpone, salt, and pepper and sauté until the cheese is melted. This whole process should not take long at all, maybe 1 minute. The point is not to stew the tomatoes, but have them retain their fresh taste. Arrange the pasta on a platter, sprinkle with Parmesan, and spoon the sauce on top. Garnish with the parsley.

Cooking on a Woodstove

When I'm down in the galley by my woodstove, folks will often reminisce about their grandmothers, or maybe mothers, cooking over a woodstove. A woodstove is something most of the cooks before us used every day, but its use is becoming a lost art. We do our best to keep it alive on the *Riggin*.

Woodstoves are ideal for soups, stews, and roasts because these dishes all lend themselves to slow, steady cooking. Woodstoves offer just that—a good, consistent heat — as long as the fire is maintained. The wood smoke provides a wonderful flavor to anything cooked in the oven, especially baked bread.

I light the stove at 4:30 a.m. to have coffee and tea water ready by 6:30 a.m. Lighting a fire in the stove is no different than lighting a campfire. Crumple newspaper or other paper, lay small pieces of kindling on the paper, and then a little larger piece on top. Crisscross the kindling and open all the dampers to provide the oxygen necessary for the fire to catch. The bigger logs don't go on until the fire is roaring along. Once it is, adding larger, rounder logs will encourage a slow and steady heat.

Once the fire is well lit, controlling the level of heat becomes the focus. When wanting to increase the heat, give it more wood and more air; this means using smaller pieces of wood and opening the dampers. When wanting to reduce the heat, close the dampers and add big pieces of wood that will take longer to burn. Apparent wind is one of the biggest challenges to cooking on a woodstove on a boat. How much wood the stove needs on a downwind day is completely different from how much it needs on a day we are tacking.

Heat on the stovetop is uneven— warmer by the firebox (where the fire is) and cooler farther away. Unlike a home stove, the temperature is not quickly adjusted at the burner, but rather by moving the pots to the warmer or cooler spots depending on how much heat is needed at the moment. The same goes for the oven, where constantly turning the pans and shifting them from the top to bottom shelves, achieves a consistent bake. It's always a race to get the insides done before the top or the bottom darkens too much. And I never forget that the whole stove gets hot!

Yeast Breads

There is nothing more tactile that the kneading of bread. The rhythmic push and pull which creates longer strands of gluten that eventually give structure to bread is, to my mind, best done by hand. A machine cannot replace the feel of dough as it goes from mottled to smooth or the knowing that develops in the mind and hands with repetition and time.

Bread By Hand

The scent of baking bread and wood smoke is a guaranteed way to get mouths watering on deck or in the galley. Of all of the dishes I make on the *Riggin*, there is little more evocative that the smell of freshly baked bread emerging from my woodstove.

There are a couple of things I focus on each time I make yeast bread by hand. Each enhances the flavor and texture of the bread.

Kneading

There is no way to over knead a loaf of bread by hand. More caution, however, is required when using a dough hook. Usually my mess cooks are asking "Am I done yet?" long before the bread is fully kneaded. The most important result of kneading is the development of gluten, which keeps the bread from collapsing. Typically kneading the dough by hand or with a dough hook 5 to 10 minutes is enough to develop the gluten proteins and to create a smooth, uniform ball that doesn't stick to the counter.

Rising

The longer it takes the dough to rise, the more flavor and texture it will have. Rising the dough in the refrigerator overnight is a sure way to develop the classic sour flavor prized in quality bread.

Proofing

I don't proof my yeast every time I use it, only because I use it so often. However, if you need to dust the top of the yeast container before opening it, then you should proof the yeast. Just place the required yeast in half of the warm water and wait 5 minutes. If it bubbles, it's alive and well. Also be sure to stir the flour, salt, and yeast briefly first, then add the remaining ingredients. This insures that the salt and yeast don't end up in clumps next to each other which will retard the yeast development.

Flour vs. Water

When making bread, it's better to use a fixed amount of flour and then add water to adjust the texture of the dough rather than add additional flour after you've mixed everything else. Adding more flour changes the ratio of all the other ingredients to the flour, and therefore changes the flavor. Water doesn't add or subtract flavor. I do use flour to dust the counter top when I'm kneading, but I make sure that I don't need to add a whole cup of flour to get the dough to not be sticky. Better to have not added so much water.

Steam

Creating steam in an oven allows bread to rise higher and form a crisper, thicker crust. In my woodstove on the boat, I toss warm water onto the oven bottom just after sliding the bread in and quickly closing the oven door. There are two ways I've found that work to create steam in a home oven. The best method is to always have a skillet filled with rocks on the floor of the oven. Tossing a cup of water into the skillet generates more steam — like a sauna — and keeps it contained. Failing this, 3 to 4 cubes of ice thrown into a pan on the oven floor works too.

Flour

I'm a King Arthur Flour fan. We use 50 pounds of it per week. In addition, as flours have become more easily sourced, we've added specialty flours to the boat's pantry to create the individual breads we now serve on board, most of them also arriving in 50 pound bags.

Note about bread machines: While I always champion hand-kneaded, hand-shaped, woodstove or oven-baked bread, I would also choose homemade over store-bought any day. If a machine gets you homemade, healthy bread rather than bread filled with preservatives, then so be it. Go to www.athomeatsea.com/breadmachine for recipes adjusted for a Zojirushi bread machine.

Crusty Peasant Bread

Makes 2 large or 4 small loaves

1½ tablespoons instant yeast
2 teaspoons table salt
5 cups all-purpose flour
2 cups warm water
2 tablespoons extra virgin olive oil
cornmeal for dusting

Combine the yeast, salt, and flour in a large bowl. Stir in all the remaining ingredients, reserving ¼ cup water. Mix thoroughly and add the reserved water if needed. Knead for 5 to 10 minutes or until smooth. Transfer the dough to a lightly oiled bowl, cover, and set aside in a warm, draft-free place to rise for 1 hour or until doubled.

Preheat oven to 400°F. Turn the dough out onto a floured surface, divide the dough into the number of loaves you plan to make, and shape them into French-style loaves. Dust a baking sheet with cornmeal and place the loaves onto the sheet. Cover and allow to rise again. When the loaves have nearly doubled, make three diagonal slashes on each loaf with a very sharp knife. Place the pans in the oven, throw a cup of water over hot stones set in a pan in the bottom of the oven to generate steam and quickly close the oven door. Bake for 30 to 40 minutes or until an internal-read thermometer registers 190°F.

Variations
Caramelized Onion: When shaping the dough, divide and shape the dough into 4 rectangles. Add 1 cup of caramelized onion to the surface of each rectangle and roll up into a log. Pinch the ends and place onto a baking sheet. Rise and bake as above.
Roasted Red Pepper and Rosemary: Add 2 cups roasted red peppers and 2 tablespoons minced fresh rosemary to the dough.
Kalamata Olive and Roasted Garlic: Add 1½ cups pitted Kalamata olives and ½ cup roasted garlic cloves to the dough.

Focaccia
4 to 6 tablespoons extra virgin olive oil (for both the pan and the top of the bread)
coarse sea salt
several grinds fresh black pepper

Instead of shaping into loaves, divide the dough in half, and with your hands press into two oiled, rimmed baking sheets. If the dough fights you, (you'll know because it keeps shrinking back when you stretch it), just let it rest for 5 minutes and continue until it reaches the edge of the baking sheet. Oil the top of the dough and let it rise in a warm spot until doubled. Press your fingers quickly into the dough all over the surface as if you were playing the piano and then sprinkle with salt and pepper. Bake for 35 minutes or until an internal-read thermometer registers 190°F.

Garlic Knots

½ Crusty Peasant Bread recipe (page 140)

2 tablespoons salted butter

2 tablespoons extra virgin olive oil

2 teaspoons minced garlic; about 2 cloves

½ teaspoon coarse sea salt

several grinds of fresh black pepper

½ ounce grated Romano cheese; ¼ cup lightly packed

Instead of shaping into loaves, roll the dough into 4 long logs and cut each log into 5 equal lengths. Roll again briefly and then tie into a loose knot. Cover and allow to rise again until doubled.

Preheat oven to 400°F. Combine the butter, oil, garlic, salt, and pepper in a small bowl and set aside. Follow instruction above for baking. Reduce baking time to 20 minutes. Transfer the hot knots to a large bowl, toss with the butter mixture, and sprinkle with Romano. Serve warm.

Jiffy Oatmeal Bread

Makes 2 loaves

1$\frac{1}{2}$ cups boiling water
1 cup quick-cooking oats
2 tablespoons instant yeast
5$\frac{1}{2}$ cups all-purpose flour
4 teaspoons table salt
$\frac{1}{2}$ cup molasses
$\frac{1}{3}$ cup canola oil
1$\frac{1}{2}$ cups evaporated milk
1 large egg

Mix the boiling water and oatmeal together in a small bowl and set aside to cool. Combine the dry ingredients in a separate, larger bowl. Add the oatmeal along with the remaining ingredients. Mix thoroughly and Knead for 5 to 10 minutes or until smooth. Transfer the dough to a lightly oiled bowl, cover, and set aside in a warm, draft-free place to rise for 1 hour until doubled.

Preheat oven to 350°F. Lightly grease 2, 8$\frac{1}{2}$- x 4$\frac{1}{2}$-inch bread pans. Turn the dough out onto a floured surface, form 2 loaves, and place them in the bread pans. Cover and allow to rise again until doubled. Place the pans in the oven, throw a cup of water over hot stones set in a pan in the bottom of the oven to generate steam and quickly close the oven door. Bake for 40 to 45 minutes or until an internal-read thermometer registers 190°F.

Anadama Bread

Makes 3 loaves

4$\frac{1}{2}$ cups boiling water
1$\frac{1}{4}$ cups cornmeal (plus extra for the bread pans)
2$\frac{1}{2}$ tablespoons instant yeast
1$\frac{1}{2}$ tablespoons table salt
4$\frac{1}{2}$ cups all-purpose flour
4$\frac{1}{2}$ cups whole wheat flour
1 cup molasses
$\frac{1}{3}$ cup canola oil (plus extra for the bowl)

Mix the boiling water and cornmeal together in a small bowl and set aside to cool. Combine the dry ingredients in a separate, larger bowl. Add the cornmeal along with the remaining ingredients. Mix thoroughly and add up to $^3/_4$ cup water as needed. Knead for 5 to 10 minutes or until smooth. Transfer the dough to a lightly oiled bowl, cover, and set aside in a warm, draft-free place to rise for 1 hour or until doubled.

Preheat oven to 375°F. Lightly grease 3, $8^1/_2$- x $4^1/_2$-inch bread pans and sprinkle them with cornmeal. Turn the dough out onto a floured surface, form 3 loaves, and place them in the bread pans. Cover and allow to rise again until doubled. Place the pans in the oven, throw a cup of water over hot stones set in a pan in the bottom of the oven to generate steam and quickly close the oven door. Bake for 45 to 50 minutes or until an internal-read thermometer registers 190°F.

Whole Wheat Walnut Bread

Makes 2 loaves

3 cups whole wheat flour
3 cups all-purpose flour
1 tablespoon instant yeast
1 tablespoon table salt
1 tablespoon firmly packed light brown sugar
2 tablespoons molasses
2 tablespoons unsalted butter, melted
$^1/_3$ cup dry milk
$2^1/_4$ cups warm water
1 cup whole walnuts

Combine both flours, yeast, salt, and sugar in a large bowl. Stir in the remaining ingredients, reserving $^1/_4$ cup water. Add more water if needed. Knead for 5 to 10 minutes or until smooth. Transfer the dough to a lightly oiled bowl, cover, and set aside in a warm, draft-free place to rise for 1 hour or until doubled.

Preheat oven to 375°F. Divide the dough in half and shape into 2 round loaves. Place the loaves on a baking sheet. Cover and allow to rise again. When the loaves have nearly doubled, make three diagonal slashes on each loaf with a very sharp knife. Place the sheets in the oven, throw a cup of water over hot stones set in a pan in the bottom of the oven to generate steam and quickly close the oven door. Bake for 30 to 35 minutes or until an internal-read thermometer registers 190°F.

Kindergarten Rolls

When the girls were little, they made this bread at school all the time. We took to making it at home as well. Makes 2 dozen rolls

1$\frac{1}{2}$ tablespoons dry yeast
$\frac{3}{4}$ cup warm water
1 stick ($\frac{1}{2}$ cup) unsalted butter, room temperature
5 tablespoons honey
1 tablespoon table salt
3 cups warm whole milk
4 to 5 cups whole wheat flour
4 to 5 cups all-purpose flour

Mix the yeast, water, butter, honey, salt, and milk in a large bowl. Stir in the flour and mix it in with a wooden spoon. You can add other secret ingredients, like raisins, oats, cinnamon, rye and/or nuts. Cover and set in a warm place to rise for 10 to 15 minutes.

Preheat oven to 350°F. Oil a rimmed baking sheet. Turn the dough out onto a floured surface and knead for 5 to 10 minutes. When the dough becomes very smooth and elastic, form it into rolls. Place the rolls onto the prepared baking sheet. If you have time, you can let them rise again, covered. Bake the rolls for about 20 minutes or until an internal-read thermometer registers 190°F.

Sunflower Millet Bread

Makes 2 loaves

1$\frac{1}{2}$ cups water
1 cup raw millet
2$\frac{1}{2}$ teaspoons table salt
$\frac{1}{4}$ cup ($\frac{1}{2}$ stick) unsalted butter
3 tablespoons honey
1$\frac{1}{2}$ tablespoons instant yeast
3 cup all-purpose flour
3 cups whole wheat flour
1 cup unsalted sunflower seeds
cornmeal for dusting

Bring the water to a boil in a small sauce pan and add the millet, salt, butter, and honey. Reduce heat and simmer for about 15 minutes or until all the water is absorbed. Cool until lukewarm. Combine the dry ingredients in a large bowl. Add the millet mixture. Mix thoroughly and add up to 1 cup warm water as needed. Knead for 5 to 10 minutes or until smooth. Transfer the dough to a lightly oiled bowl, cover, and place in a warm place to rise for 1 hour or until doubled.

Preheat oven to 350°F. Turn the dough out onto a floured surface, divide the dough in half, and shape into 2, French-style loaves. Dust a baking sheet with cornmeal and place the loaves on the sheet. Cover and allow to rise again. When the loaves have nearly doubled, make three diagonal slashes on each loaf with a very sharp knife. Place the pans in the oven, throw a cup of water over hot stones set in a pan in the bottom of the oven to generate steam and quickly close the oven door. Bake for 45 to 50 minutes or until an internal-read thermometer registers 190°F.

Newfi Bread

This recipe is a favorite on many vessels in the windjammer fleet and also does well as rolls. Makes 3 loaves

8 cups all-purpose flour
2 tablespoons instant yeast
$1/2$ tablespoon table salt
3 cups warm water
2 tablespoons unsalted butter, room temperature
    (plus extra for the bread pans)
1 cup molasses

Combine the dry ingredients in a large bowl. Stir in all the remaining ingredients, reserving $1/4$ cup water. Mix thoroughly and add more water if needed. Knead for 5 to 10 minutes or until smooth. Transfer the dough to a lightly oiled bowl, cover, cover, and place in a warm place to rise for 1 hour or until doubled.

Preheat oven to 375°F. Lightly grease 3, $8^{1}/_{2}$- x $4^{1}/_{2}$-inch bread pans. Turn the dough out onto a floured surface, form 3 loaves, and place them in the bread pans. Cover and allow to rise again until doubled. Place the pans in the oven, throw a cup of water over hot stones set in a pan in the bottom of the oven to generate steam and quickly close the oven door. Bake for 40 to 45 minutes or until an internal-read thermometer registers 190°F.

Jim's Raisin Bread

Jim was a true Maine character. We met him when we first came to Maine. He panned for gold in the Camden Hills, taught me how to upholster my first chair, and has done just about everything else in between including baking bread. He gave me this recipe — it's easy, delicious, and it always works.
Makes 2 loaves

8 cups all-purpose flour
1$\frac{1}{2}$ tablespoons instant yeast
1 tablespoon table salt
3$\frac{1}{2}$ cups warm water
$\frac{1}{2}$ cup canola oil
$\frac{1}{3}$ cup sugar
2 cups raisins
1 large egg

Combine the dry ingredients in a large bowl. Stir in all the remaining ingredients, reserving $\frac{1}{4}$ cup water. Mix thoroughly and add more water if needed. Knead for 5 to 10 minutes or until smooth. Transfer the dough to a lightly oiled bowl, cover, and set aside in a warm, draft-free place to rise for 1 hour or until doubled.

Preheat oven to 350°F. Lightly grease 2, 8$\frac{1}{2}$- x 4$\frac{1}{2}$-inch bread pans. Turn the dough out onto a floured surface, form 2 loaves, and place them in the bread pans. Cover and allow to rise again until doubled. Place the pans in the oven, throw a cup of water over hot stones set in a pan in the bottom of the oven to generate steam and quickly close the oven door. Bake for 35 to 40 minutes or until an internal-read thermometer registers 190°F.

Variations
Cinnamon Roasted Pear: Add 2 teaspoons ground cinnamon and replace the raisins with roasted pear (or apple) slices.
Cardamom: Omit raisins and add 2 teaspoons ground cardamom.

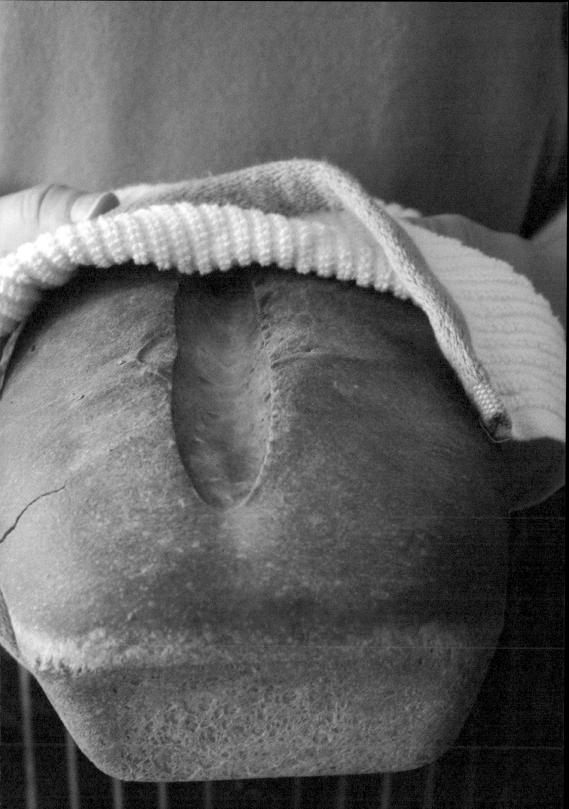

Quick Breads

Golden butter slathered on warm biscuits just from the oven and then topped with a dollop of homemade jam reminds me of home, my mom, and my grandma. The original family recipe is on an index card, now tattered and stained, in my grandma's handwriting. Each time I roll out biscuits I feel the ghost of her hands laying over mine, guiding me.

Baking Ethos

There are two kinds of people who create good food: cooks and bakers. If you are a cook, you see recipes as guidelines and something to easily change. You are not a rule follower. If you are a baker at heart, then recipes are a formula to follow. I am the former and have a really hard time doing the later. So it is in the spirit of creativity and fun that I encourage you to use these recipes as a starting point and why many of them have variations on the original theme. Don't worry though if you don't happen to have a woodstove handy at home. All of these recipes have been tested in a home kitchen.

Method

Due to time, space, and other constraints while cooking onboard, I've created a method for streamlining the process for making biscuits, quick breads, and muffins.

A lot of true bakers, which I've just admitted I am not, will tell you that you need to use several bowls to make a few simple muffins. One for the pre-sifted, pre-measured flour, one for the creamed ingredients, one for a finger bowl... Not me. On the boat and at home, we have limited resources in water, energy, and/or time and (I know you can appreciate this) we want as few dirty dishes as possible. With that in mind, the ingredients are broken down into three groups: creamed, dry, and liquid.

If there is creaming to be done, it gets done first; butter and sugar creamed in a big bowl, then eggs and sometimes a few other ingredients get sifted into the bowl with the creamed ingredients. Add any additional liquid and mix it all up. One bowl, no lumps.

If the recipe does not call for creaming, then the dry ingredients get sifted into a large bowl. Make a well in the center for all of the wet ingredients. Mix from the center and work out. Again, one bowl, no lumps.

The dry ingredients don't get sifted beforehand— too many dishes. I've made whatever adjustments need to be made to reduce the amount of flour so the recipes come out properly. The one thing I stick to religiously is leveling off the measuring cups and spoons with a knife or anything flat. This makes a big difference in the final product and also in the ability to make the taste and texture consistent every time.

What Counter Space?

The galley of the *Riggin* has about 3 feet of counter space (give or take a few inches), hence the need to streamline baking processes. I'm often asked how I manage to prepare meals for 30 people all summer long on such a small space. One guest, whose wife was angling for a new kitchen, even came to measure the exact amount of counter space so that he could use this information as his rebuttal. I'm not sure how well that worked in the end, but I did discover how little space I really have!

Organization

I am not by nature a strictly organized person, but I do happen to like efficiency. Cooking well requires that a person have some semblance of organization before beginning, this is just as true in baking as it is in cooking. Chefs call this "mise en place" or everything in its place. Preparedness takes a level of stress away and insures consistent success. It also helps that my mess cook and the ambitious guests do a lot of the chopping for me so that I can keep the pots rolling along.

Baking Powder Biscuits

This is a recipe my grandma passed on to me through my mom. My grandmother used shortening, and maybe even lard. Currently, shortening is out and butter is in, but to honor the history of the recipe, I've left shortening as an ingredient. It is a one to one replacement to substitute butter. Makes 12 biscuits

2 cups all-purpose flour
2 teaspoons baking powder
$^1/_2$ teaspoon table salt
$^1/_4$ cup shortening
$^3/_4$ cup whole milk

Preheat oven to 450°F. Measure the flour, baking powder, and salt into a sifter set in a medium bowl. This is an important step because you want to add air to the mixture so the biscuits are as fluffy as possible. Use a pastry cutter to cut the shortening into the mixture until it resembles a coarse meal. Stir in any additional dry ingredients

here (see below). Add milk and any additional wet ingredients (see below), stirring until a soft dough forms. It is important to not overmix; you'll hard tack instead of fluffy biscuits. Turn out onto a floured board and knead 10 times, then STOP! Roll or pat out the dough until it is ½-inch thick. Cut with a floured 2-inch biscuit cutter. Transfer the biscuits to an ungreased baking sheet. Bake for 12 to 15 minutes or until golden brown.

Variations

Lemon and Herb Biscuits
To the basic recipe add:
1 tablespoon lemon zest; about 1 lemon
1 teaspoon fresh lemon juice
3 tablespoons of fresh herbs such as chives, chive blossoms, lemon thyme, thyme, rosemary, and/or lavender

Parmesan and Black Pepper Biscuits
To the basic recipe add:
several grinds fresh black pepper
½ teaspoon baking soda
2 ounces grated Parmesan cheese; about 1 cup lightly packed
1 large egg
a little extra milk if needed

Roquefort and Walnut Biscuits
To the basic recipe add:
4 ounces crumbled Roquefort cheese; about 1 cup
½ cup finely chopped walnuts or pecans
⅛ teaspoon cayenne
1 pinch paprika
1 large egg yolk
2 tablespoons heavy cream

Jack and Jalapeño Biscuits
To the basic recipe add:
2 ounces grated Monterey Jack cheese; about 1 cup
1 tablespoon seeded and minced jalapeño pepper

Poppy Seed and Orange
To the basic recipe add:
2 tablespoons poppy seeds
2 tablespoons orange zest; about 1 orange

Cheddar Cheese Biscuits

Makes 12 biscuits

2 cups all-purpose flour
1 tablespoon sugar
2 $\frac{1}{2}$ teaspoons baking powder
$\frac{1}{2}$ teaspoon baking soda
$\frac{1}{2}$ teaspoon table salt
several grinds fresh black pepper
6 tablespoons ($\frac{3}{4}$ stick) unsalted butter, chilled and cut into $\frac{1}{2}$-inch cubes
5 ounces grated cheddar cheese; about 1$\frac{1}{4}$ cups lightly packed
$\frac{3}{4}$ to 1 cup buttermilk
1 large egg
1 tablespoon whole milk
poppy seeds for garnish

Preheat oven to 400°F. Combine the flour, sugar, baking powder, baking soda, salt, and pepper in a large mixing bowl. Use a pastry cutter to cut the butter into the mixture until it resembles a fine meal. Add the cheese and then the buttermilk just until the dough binds together. Do not overmix. Turn out onto a floured surface and knead gently until combined, about 10 turns. Pat the dough out to a $\frac{3}{4}$-inch thickness. Cut into biscuits with a 2-inch biscuit cutter. Transfer the biscuits to an ungreased baking sheet. Whisk together the egg and milk in a small bowl and brush over the biscuits with a pastry brush. Sprinkle with poppy seeds. Bake for 10 to 15 minutes or until golden brown.

Herb Cheese Bread

Makes 1 loaf

$\frac{1}{2}$ cup firmly packed light brown sugar
2 tablespoons unsalted butter, room temperature
$\frac{2}{3}$ cup buttermilk
3 ounces grated cheddar cheese; about $\frac{2}{3}$ cup lightly packed
$\frac{2}{3}$ cup cottage cheese
2 large eggs
3 cups all-purpose flour
1 teaspoon baking soda
1 teaspoon baking powder
1 teaspoon table salt

1 teaspoon dried dill
$^1/_2$ teaspoon dried basil
$^1/_2$ teaspoon dried tarragon
$^1/_2$ teaspoon dried oregano

Preheat oven to 350°F. Lightly grease an $8^1/_2$- x $4^1/_2$-inch bread pan. Cream the sugar and butter in a medium-sized bowl with a wooden spoon. Add the buttermilk, cheeses, and eggs and combine. Sift in the dry ingredients, add the herbs, and stir until just combined. Spoon the mixture into the prepared pan. Bake for 45 to 55 minutes or until a toothpick inserted into the center comes out clean and the center springs back when lightly pressed. Cool in the pan on a wire rack for 5 minutes before removing.

Golden Northern Cornbread

Makes 9 pieces

1 cup all-purpose flour
2 teaspoons baking powder
$^1/_2$ teaspoon baking soda
4 teaspoons sugar
$^1/_2$ teaspoon table salt
1 cup yellow or white stone-ground cornmeal
2 large eggs
$^2/_3$ cup buttermilk
$^2/_3$ cup whole milk
2 tablespoons unsalted butter, melted (plus more for the pan)

Preheat the oven to 400°F. Lightly grease a cast-iron skillet or 9- x 9-inch baking pan. Sift the flour, baking powder, baking soda, sugar, and salt into a medium-sized bowl. Add the cornmeal. Make a well in the center of the dry ingredients and add the rest of the ingredients. Stir until just combined. Pour the batter into the prepared pan. Bake for 20 to 25 minutes or until a toothpick comes out clean and the center springs back when lightly pressed. Cool in the pan on a wire rack for 5 minutes. Cut into squares and serve warm.

Irish Soda Bread

This is another recipe passed down through the women in my family. My grandma favored currents and caraway seeds and my mom made it unadorned. Either way, it's a versatile recipe. Makes 2 loaves or 1 large loaf

4 cups all-purpose flour
2 teaspoons table salt
1½ teaspoons baking soda
1½ teaspoons cream of tartar
½ cup sugar
1¾ cups buttermilk

Preheat oven to 350°F. Sift the flour, salt, baking soda, cream of tartar, and sugar in a large bowl. Make a well in the center of the flour and add the milk. Stir until a ball just forms and turn onto floured board. Knead until combined (about 5 turns). Cut the dough in half and shape into two 6-inch round loaves. Place the loaves on a baking sheet. Make two perpendicular cuts on top of the loaves in the shape of a cross. Bake for 40 minutes or until a toothpick comes out clean.

Variations
Fennel and Raisin: Add 2 tablespoons fennel seeds and 1 cup raisins.
Caraway and Currants: Add 2 tablespoons caraway seeds and 1 cup currants.
Whole Wheat and Flax Seed: Replace 1 cup all-purpose flour with whole wheat flour. Add 3 tablespoons whole flax seeds.
Stilton and Chives: Reduce the buttermilk by 1 tablespoon. Add 1 cup crumbled Stilton and ½ cup minced chives.

Scones

Makes 12 scones

2 cups all-purpose flour
2 teaspoons baking powder
$^1/_4$ cup sugar
$^1/_2$ teaspoon table salt
6 tablespoons ($^3/_4$ stick) unsalted butter, chilled and cut into $^1/_2$-inch cubes
$^1/_2$ cup raisins
$^1/_2$ cup whole milk
1 large egg

Preheat oven to 375°F. Sift the flour, baking powder, sugar, and salt into a medium-sized bowl. This is an important step because you want to add air to the mixture so the scones are as light as possible. Use a pastry cutter to cut the butter into the mixture until it resembles a coarse meal. Stir in the raisins. Add the milk, egg, and any additional wet ingredients, stirring until a soft dough forms. Add more milk if needed. It is important to not overmix; you'll get hard tack instead of scones. Turn out onto a floured board and knead 10 times, then STOP! Roll or pat the dough until it is $^1/_2$-inch thick. Cut with a floured 1$^1/_2$-inch biscuit cutter. Transfer the biscuits to an ungreased baking sheet. Bake for 12 to 15 minutes or until golden brown.

To make one large scone
Place the dough on a baking sheet and shape it into a circle about 6 to 7 inches in diameter. Brush the top with a tiny bit of half and half and sprinkle with sugar. Score the "pie" into 8 to 10 pieces. Increase the baking time to 15 to 20 minutes.

Variations
Apricot Ginger: Replace raisins with chopped dried apricots and crystallized ginger.
Cranberry Almond: Replace raisins with dried cranberries and chopped almonds.
Brown Sugar and Date: Replace the sugar with brown sugar and the raisins with minced dates. Sprinkle the top with demerara sugar before baking.
Sour Cherry and Walnut: Replace the raisins with sour cherries and add $^1/_2$ cup chopped walnuts.

Mom and Grandma's Brown Bread

This was my grandmother's recipe. The original recipe called for graham flour and sour milk. I've substituted whole wheat flour and buttermilk. Makes 1 loaf

2 tablespoons unsalted butter, room temperature
½ cup firmly packed light brown sugar
2 cups buttermilk
2 large eggs
3 tablespoons molasses
1 cup all-purpose flour
2 cups whole wheat flour
1 teaspoon baking soda
1 teaspoon baking powder
1 teaspoon table salt

Preheat oven to 375°F. Lightly grease an 8½- x 4½-inch bread pan. Cream together the butter and sugar with a wooden spoon in a medium-sized bowl. Add the milk, eggs, and molasses and stir until just combined. Stir in the flours, baking soda, baking powder, and salt. Pour into the prepared pan, and let it sit 20 to 30 minutes. Bake for 45 minutes to 1 hour or until a toothpick inserted into the center comes out clean and the center springs back when lightly pressed. Cool in the pan on a wire rack for 5 minutes before removing.

Out of Buttermilk? The recipes I have from my grandma all call for sour milk. When my mom uses these same recipes, she uses buttermilk. On the boat, to simplify shopping, I buy one kind of milk— whole milk. When I need buttermilk for a recipe, I add 1 to 2 tablespoons of lemon juice or cider vinegar to a little less than 1 cup of milk and let it sit to curdle for a couple of minutes before using.

Crossroads Banana Bread

Crossroads was the specialty deli at my alma mater, Michigan State University, and the original creator of this recipe. Of course there we made it in huge, stainless mixers, but one loaf at a time does nicely for a household. Makes 1 loaf

1 teaspoon fresh lemon juice
2 tablespoons buttermilk
2 cups mashed ripe bananas; about 4 bananas
1 cup sugar
$\frac{1}{2}$ cup (1 stick) unsalted butter, room temperature
2 large eggs
2 cups all-purpose flour
2 teaspoons baking powder
1 teaspoon baking soda
$\frac{1}{2}$ teaspoon table salt

Preheat oven to 350°F. Lightly grease an $8\frac{1}{2}$- x $4\frac{1}{2}$-inch bread pan. Pour the lemon juice and buttermilk over the mashed bananas in a small bowl and set aside. Cream the sugar, butter, and eggs in a medium-sized bowl with a wooden spoon or the bowl of a stand mixer with the paddle attachment. Add the milk and banana mixture. Sift the dry ingredients into the bowl and stir until just combined. Spoon the batter into the prepared pan. Bake for 1 hour and 10 minutes or until a toothpick inserted into the center comes out clean and the center springs back when lightly pressed. Cool in the pan on a wire rack for 5 minutes before removing.

Variation
Banana Chocolate Chip Cake: Add 2 cups of chocolate chips to the batter. Pour the batter into a greased 9- x 13-inch pan and bake for 35 to 45 minutes.

Blueberry Lemon Bread

Makes 1 loaf

$1\frac{1}{2}$ cups all-purpose flour
1 teaspoon baking powder
$\frac{1}{4}$ teaspoon table salt
6 tablespoons ($\frac{3}{4}$ stick) unsalted butter, room temperature
1 cup sugar
2 large eggs
2 teaspoons lemon zest; about $\frac{1}{2}$ lemon

1 teaspoon lemon extract
$^1/_2$ cup whole milk
$1^1/_2$ cups fresh Maine blueberries
3 tablespoons fresh lemon juice; about 1 lemon
$^1/_3$ cup sugar

Preheat oven to 325°F. Lightly grease an $8^1/_2$- x $4^1/_2$-inch bread pan. Sift the dry ingredients in a small bowl and set aside. Cream the butter and 1 cup of sugar in a medium-sized bowl with a wooden spoon or the bowl of a stand mixer with the paddle attachment. Add the eggs one at a time, mixing well each time. Add the lemon zest and extract. Add the sifted dry ingredients, alternating with the milk, into the sugar and egg mixture, adding the dry ingredients last. Fold in the blueberries and spoon into the prepared pan. Bake for 1 hour and 15 minutes or until a toothpick inserted into the center comes out clean and the bread springs back when lightly pressed. Whisk the lemon juice and sugar in a small bowl or sauce pan. Heat briefly until the sugar dissolves. Use a pastry brush to brush the surface of the warm bread with the glaze. Cool on a wire rack for 10 minutes before removing.

Cranberry Orange Bread

Makes 1 loaf

2 cups all-purpose flour
$^1/_2$ teaspoon table salt
$1^1/_2$ teaspoons baking powder
$^1/_2$ teaspoon baking soda
1 cup sugar
1 large egg
3 tablespoons unsalted butter, melted
$^3/_4$ cup fresh orange juice
3 tablespoons orange zest; about 1 orange
$^1/_2$ cup nuts (optional)
2 cups fresh cranberries

Preheat oven to 350°F. Lightly grease an $8^1/_2$- x $4^1/_2$-inch bread pan. Sift the dry ingredients into a medium-sized bowl. Make a well in the center of the dry ingredients and add the egg, butter, orange juice, and orange zest until just combined. Fold in the nuts and cranberries. Spoon the batter into the prepared pan. Bake for 50 minutes or until a toothpick inserted into the center comes out clean and the bread springs back when lightly pressed. Cool in the pan over a wire rack for 5 minutes before removing.

Lorraine's Nectarine Blueberry Bread

Lorraine, one of the owners of the Schooner Victory Chimes, *gave this recipe to me when I was running the galley for them. It's still one of my favorites.* Makes 1 loaf

$^3/_4$ cup sugar (plus 1 tablespoon for the topping)
5 tablespoons unsalted butter, room temperature
2 large eggs
$1^1/_2$ cups all-purpose flour
$^1/_2$ teaspoon ground allspice
$^1/_4$ teaspoon baking soda
1 teaspoon orange zest
1 medium nectarine, peeled and cut into $^1/_4$-inch pieces
1 cup fresh blueberries
$^2/_3$ cup chopped almonds
1 tablespoon sugar

Preheat oven to 350°F. Lightly grease an 8^1/$_2$- x 4^1/$_2$-inch bread pan. Cream ^{3}/$_4$ cup of sugar and the butter in a medium-sized bowl with a wooden spoon or the bowl of a stand mixer with the paddle attachment. Add the eggs and mix well. Sift all the dry ingredients into the bowl and stir until just combined. Gently stir in the fruit. Pour the batter into the prepared pan. Mix the almonds and 1 tablespoon sugar together in a small bowl and sprinkle the mixture over the batter. Bake for 1 hour or until a toothpick inserted into the center comes out clean and the center springs back when lightly pressed. Cool in the pan on a wire rack for 5 minutes before removing.

Pumpkin Bread

When I make this for a special afternoon tea, I replace ^{1}/$_3$ cup orange juice with ^{1}/$_3$ cup Grand Marnier. Makes 2 loaves

^{2}/$_3$ cup (1^1/$_3$ sticks) unsalted butter, room temperature
2 ^{2}/$_3$ cups sugar
4 large eggs
1 (16-ounce) can pumpkin puree
^{2}/$_3$ cup fresh orange juice (or ^{1}/$_3$ cup orange juice
    and ^{1}/$_3$ cup Grand Marnier)
1 cup currants
3^1/$_3$ cups all-purpose flour
2 teaspoons baking soda
1^1/$_2$ teaspoons table salt
^{1}/$_2$ teaspoon baking powder
1 teaspoon ground cinnamon
1 teaspoon ground cloves

Preheat the oven to 350°F. Lightly grease 2, 8^1/$_2$- x 4^1/$_2$-inch bread pans. Cream the sugar and butter in a medium-sized bowl with a wooden spoon or the bowl of a stand mixer with the paddle attachment. Add the eggs, pumpkin, orange juice, optional liquor, and optional currants and mix well. Sift the dry ingredients into the bowl and stir until just combined. Pour the batter into the prepared pans. Bake for 55 minutes to 1 hour or until a toothpick inserted into the center comes out clean and the center springs back when lightly pressed. Cool in the pan on a wire rack for 5 minutes before removing.

Variation
Pumpkin Raisin Walnut: Replace currants with raisins and add chopped walnuts.

Poppy Seed Bread

This recipe is based on one given to me by CIA alumna and former schooner chef, Dana Degenhardt.
Makes 2 loaves

Bread
3 cups all-purpose flour
1½ teaspoons table salt
1½ teaspoons baking powder
2½ cups sugar
1½ cups whole milk
3 large eggs
1 cup canola oil
5 tablespoons whole dry poppy seeds
2 teaspoons vanilla extract
2 teaspoons almond extract

Glaze
2½ tablespoons sugar
1 tablespoon fresh orange juice
⅛ teaspoon vanilla extract
⅛ teaspoon almond extract
2 teaspoons unsalted butter

Bread
Preheat oven to 350°F. Lightly grease 2, 8½- x 4½-inch bread pans. Sift the flour, salt, baking powder, and sugar into a large bowl or the bowl of a stand mixer with the paddle attachment. Add the remaining bread ingredients and stir until just combined. Divide the batter evenly between the 2 prepared pans. Bake for 1 hour and 15 minutes or until a toothpick inserted into the center comes out clean and the center springs back when lightly pressed.

Glaze
Whisk the glaze ingredients in a small sauce pan or bowl. Heat briefly until the sugar dissolves. Use a pastry brush to brush the surface of the warm bread with the glaze. Cool in the pan on a wire rack for 10 minutes before removing.

Variations
Lemon Poppy Seed Bread: Replace the almond extract with lemon extract in both the batter and the glaze. Add lemon zest to the batter.

Orange Poppy Seed Bread: Replace almond extract with orange extract in both the batter and the glaze. Add orange zest to the batter.
Cake: Bake in a 9- x 13-inch pan. Reduce baking time to 35 to 40 minutes.
Cupcakes: Bake in a prepared 12-cup muffin pan. Reduce baking time to 15 to 20 minutes. Instead of the glaze, frost the cupcakes with a strawberry cream cheese frosting or a lemon butter frosting.

Zucchini Bread

Makes 1 loaf

3 large eggs
1 cup canola oil
2 cups sugar
2 cups grated zucchini; about 1 zucchini
2 teaspoons vanilla extract
3 cups all-purpose flour
1 teaspoon baking soda
$\frac{1}{2}$ teaspoon baking powder
1 teaspoon table salt
1 teaspoon ground cinnamon
$\frac{1}{2}$ cup coarsely chopped nuts (walnuts, pecans, etc.)

Preheat oven to 325°F. Lightly grease an $8\frac{1}{2}$- x $4\frac{1}{2}$-inch bread pans. Combine the eggs, oil, sugar, zucchini, and vanilla in a large bowl. Sift the dry ingredients into the bowl and stir until just combined. Fold in the nuts. Spoon the batter into the prepared pan. Bake for 55 minutes to 1 hour or until a toothpick comes out clean and the bread springs back when lightly pressed. Cool in the pan on a wire rack for 5 minutes before removing.

Variations
Summer Squash or Carrot Bread: Replace the grated zucchini with grated summer squash or carrots.
Double Chocolate Zucchini Bread: Replace $\frac{1}{2}$ cup of flour with cocoa powder, the cinnamon with espresso powder, and the nuts with 1 cup chocolate chips.
Cake: Bake in a 9- x 9-inch pan. Reduce baking time to 25 to 30 minutes.
Cupcakes: Bake in a prepared 12-cup muffin pan. Reduce baking time to 15 to 20 minutes. Instead of the glaze, frost the cupcakes with a cardamom cream cheese frosting or an orange butter frosting.

Spiced Apple Muffins

Makes 12 muffins

$^{1}/_{4}$ cup raisins
$^{1}/_{4}$ cup currants
$^{1}/_{4}$ cup rum
2 cups all-purpose flour
$^{1}/_{2}$ teaspoon table salt
$^{1}/_{2}$ teaspoon baking soda
$^{1}/_{2}$ teaspoon ground cinnamon
pinch ground cardamom
$^{3}/_{4}$ cup canola oil
1 cup sugar
1 large egg
$^{1}/_{2}$ teaspoon vanilla extract
2 small apples, peeled, cored, and diced; about $1^{1}/_{2}$ cups
$^{1}/_{2}$ cup coarsely chopped walnuts

Soak the raisins and currants in the rum for at least 1 hour or as long as overnight.

Preheat oven to 350°F. Lightly grease a 12-cup muffin pan or line with paper liners. Sift the dry ingredients into a medium-sized bowl. Make a well in the center and add the rest of the ingredients including the raisins, currants, and rum. Stir until just combined. Fill muffin cups two-thirds full with the batter. Bake for 20 to 25 minutes or until a toothpick comes out clean and the muffins spring back when lightly pressed. Remove the muffins from the pan to cool on a wire rack.

Variation
Spiced Pear, Cranberry, and Sherry: Replace apples with pears; raisins and currants with dried cranberries; and rum with sherry.

Applesauce Muffins

Makes 12 muffins

2 cups all-purpose flour
1 tablespoon baking powder
$^{1}/_{2}$ cup firmly packed light brown sugar
$^{1}/_{2}$ teaspoon baking soda
$^{1}/_{2}$ teaspoon table salt
$^{1}/_{2}$ teaspoon ground cinnamon

$^1/_2$ teaspoon nutmeg
1 cup applesauce
$^1/_4$ cup whole milk
1 large egg
$^1/_4$ cup ($^1/_2$ stick) unsalted butter, melted
$^1/_2$ cup raisins

Preheat oven to 375°F. Lightly grease a 12-cup muffin pan or line with paper liners. Sift the dry ingredients into a medium-sized bowl. Make a well in the center and add the rest of the ingredients. Stir until just combined. Fill the prepared muffin cups two-thirds full with the batter. Bake 15 to 20 minutes or until a toothpick inserted into the center comes out clean and the muffins spring back when lightly pressed. Remove the muffins from the pan to cool on a wire rack.

Blueberry Muffins

I use this recipe as a base for many different kinds of muffins. It's very forgiving and tasty too.
Makes 12 muffins

2 cups all-purpose flour
$^2/_3$ cup sugar
1 tablespoon baking powder
$^3/_4$ teaspoon table salt
$^1/_3$ cup canola oil
2 large eggs
$^2/_3$ cup whole milk
1$^1/_3$ cups fresh Maine blueberries

Preheat oven to 350°F. Lightly grease a 12-cup muffin pan or line with paper liners. Sift the dry ingredients into a medium-sized bowl. Make a well in the center of the dry ingredients and add the oil, eggs, and milk. Stir until just combined. Gently fold in the blueberries. Fill the muffin cups two-thirds full. Bake for 15 to 20 minutes or until a toothpick inserted into the center comes out clean and the muffins spring back when lightly pressed. Remove the muffins from the pan to cool on a wire rack.

Variations
Pumpkin, Honey, and Walnut: Reduce the milk to $^1/_3$ cup, add 2 tablespoons honey, and 1 cup pumpkin puree with the other liquid ingredients. Stir in $^3/_4$ cup chopped walnuts instead of the blueberries.
Other Variations: Replace the blueberries with dried cranberries or apricots; raisins; or chocolate chips.

Sweet Endings

At anchor, the awning is up, the decks are cleared, and dinner is over. Jon and I sit, shoulders touching, and look out over the harbor to watch the sunset with our guests as we enjoy our after-dinner coffee and dessert. We breathe in the satisfaction of a day well-lived and—shared.

Brownies

I've adapted this recipe from my friend Ellen's brownie recipe. It has a deep, rich flavor and the espresso powder and the almond extract are the secret ingredients! Makes 24 brownies

8 ounces (8 squares) unsweetened chocolate
1 cup (2 sticks) unsalted butter
5 large eggs
1 tablespoon vanilla extract
1 teaspoon almond extract
$1/4$ teaspoon table salt
$2^1/2$ tablespoons espresso powder or instant coffee
$3^3/4$ cups sugar
1 cup walnuts (optional)
$1^2/3$ cups all-purpose flour

Preheat oven to 375°F. Lightly grease a 9- x 13-inch baking pan. Melt the chocolate and butter in a double boiler until the chocolate is almost melted. Remove from heat and stir occasionally until the chocolate is completely melted and cooled to room temperature. Combine the eggs, extracts, salt, espresso powder, and sugar in a large bowl with a wooden spoon or in the bowl of a stand mixer with the paddle attachment. Add the chocolate mixture and the walnuts. Sift in the flour and mix until blended. Spread the batter evenly in the prepared pan. Bake for 35 minutes or until a toothpick comes out clean and the brownies spring back when lightly pressed. Cool in the pan slightly on a wire rack and cut into squares while still warm.

Congo Bars

Makes 24 bars

$2^1/3$ cups firmly packed light brown sugar
$3/4$ cup ($1^1/2$ sticks) unsalted butter
$1/2$ teaspoon vanilla extract
3 large eggs
$2^1/4$ cups all-purpose flour
$2^1/2$ teaspoons baking powder $1/2$ teaspoon table salt
6 ounces bittersweet chocolate chips; 1 cup chips
1 cup chopped walnuts

Preheat oven to 350°F. Lightly grease a 9- x 13-inch pan. Melt the brown sugar and butter over low heat in a medium saucepan. Cool slightly, add the vanilla, then beat in the eggs. Stir in the flour, baking powder, and salt. Add the chocolate chips and walnuts. Spread the dough evenly into the prepared pan and bake for 30 minutes. If a toothpick inserted into the center comes out slightly gooey, this is okay. Cool in the pan slightly on a wire rack and cut into squares while still warm.

Variation
Drunken Pepper Pie: Add 1 teaspoon ancho chili powder to the batter. Transfer the batter to a blind baked pie crust and bake for 25 to 30 minutes. Serve with whipped cream.

Bailey's Irish Cream Chocolate Mint Bars

This is one that my family would make every Christmas, sans Bailey's when we were little. My brothers and I could eat a pan of these in no time flat. It's really no different on the Riggin— *they disappear quickly.* Makes 24 bars

Bars
$^2/_3$ cup ($1^1/_3$ sticks) unsalted butter
4 ounces (4 squares) unsweetened chocolate
2 cups firmly packed light brown sugar
3 large eggs
1 tablespoon Bailey's Irish Cream
1 teaspoon vanilla extract
$1^1/_4$ cups all-purpose flour
1 teaspoon baking powder
$^1/_2$ teaspoon table salt

Frosting
2 cups confectioner's sugar
$^1/_4$ cup ($^1/_2$ stick) unsalted butter, room temperature
2 tablespoons Bailey's Irish Cream
$^3/_4$ teaspoon peppermint extract

Glaze
3 ounces (3 squares) unsweetened chocolate
2 tablespoons unsalted butter

Bars
Preheat oven to 350°F. Lightly grease a 9- x 13-inch baking pan. Melt the chocolate and butter in a double boiler until the chocolate is almost melted. Remove from heat and stir occasionally until the chocolate is completely melted and cooled to room temperature. Beat in the sugar, eggs, Bailey's, and vanilla. Sift in the dry ingredients and stir until just combined. Spoon the batter into the prepared pan. Bake for 25 to 30 minutes or until a toothpick inserted into the center comes out clean and the center springs back when lightly pressed. Cool in the pan on a wire rack.

Frosting
Beat the frosting ingredients together until light and creamy and then frost the bars.

Glaze
Melt the glaze ingredients, cool slightly, and pour the glaze over the frosting. Tilt the pan to spread the glaze. Cool before cutting.

Hello Dolly Bars

We also call these Everything-But-the-Kitchen-Sink Bars because it seems every ingredient in the kitchen is in this recipe! Makes 24 bars

5 tablespoons unsalted butter, melted
3 tablespoons sugar
1½ cup graham cracker crumbs
6 ounces semisweet chocolate chips; 1 cup chips
6 ounces butterscotch chips; 1 cup chips
1 cup shredded coconut
1 cup chopped nuts (pecan, almonds, or walnuts)
1 (14-ounce) can sweetened condensed milk

Preheat oven to 350°F. Pour the melted butter into a 9- x 13-inch pan. Sprinkle the sugar and graham cracker crumbs evenly over the butter and combine. Press well into the pan. Sprinkle the chocolate chips in an even layer over the crumbs. Repeat with the butterscotch chips, coconut, and nuts. Drizzle the condensed milk evenly over the nuts. Bake for 20 minutes or until the top is bubbly. Cool in the pan slightly on a wire rack and cut into squares while still warm.

Mandel Balchen

The recipe for these beautiful wafers was given to me by former schooner chef, Dana Degenhardt. These flourless cookies are delicate and rich, perfect for an afternoon tea (and for our gluten-free selves or friends). Makes around 2 dozen

3 ounces bittersweet chocolate chips; $\frac{1}{2}$ cup chips
6 tablespoons ($\frac{3}{4}$ stick) unsalted butter, room temperature
$\frac{3}{4}$ cup confectioner's sugar
$\frac{1}{4}$ teaspoon almond extract
$\frac{3}{4}$ cup very finely ground almonds

Melt the chocolate in a double boiler until the chocolate is almost melted. Remove from heat and stir occasionally until the chocolate is completely melted and cooled to room temperature. Cream the butter and sugar in a large bowl with a wooden spoon or the bowl of a stand mixer with the paddle attachment. Stir in the melted chocolate, almond extract, and almonds. Form the dough into a ball, wrap it in plastic wrap, and chill it for 1 hour.

Preheat oven to 175°F (yes, really 175°F). To form the cookies, pinch off about 1 teaspoon of the dough, roll into a ball, and place it on an ungreased baking sheet. Space evenly apart, using 2 baking sheets. Bake for 50 minutes. Turn off the oven but leave the sheets in the closed oven for 1 hour. Gently remove the cookies from the pan.

Raspberry Bars

Makes 24 bars

$1\frac{1}{2}$ cups (3 sticks) unsalted butter, room temperature
$1\frac{1}{4}$ cups sugar
1 large egg
$2\frac{1}{4}$ cups all-purpose flour
$\frac{1}{4}$ teaspoon table salt
1 cup raspberry preserves

Preheat oven to 350°F. Butter a 9- x 13-inch baking pan. Cream the butter and sugar in a large bowl with a wooden spoon or the bowl of a stand mixer with the paddle attachment. Add the egg and then sift in the flour and salt. Press half of the dough into the prepared pan. Spread the jam evenly on top of the dough; crumble the remaining dough over the preserves as evenly as possible. Bake about 30 minutes, until the top is golden brown. Cool in the pan on a wire rack.

Variations

Raspberry Oat: Add 1 cup old-fashioned rolled oats with the flour.

Raspberry Chocolate Almond: Layer 1 cup semisweet chocolate chips and ½ cup slivered almonds on top before baking.

Orange Marmalade and White Chocolate: Replace raspberry jam with orange marmalade. Add 1 cup white chocolate chips on top before baking.

Nutella®: Replace raspberry jam with Nutella® and sprinkle with ½ cup chopped hazelnuts before baking.

Ginger Shortbread

Makes 8 to 10 pieces

1 cup (2 sticks) unsalted butter, room temperature
1 cup confectioner's sugar
2 teaspoons vanilla extract
2 cups all-purpose flour
$1/4$ teaspoon table salt
$1/4$ cup minced crystallized ginger

Preheat oven to 350°F. Cream the butter and sugar in a medium-sized bowl with a wooden spoon or the bowl of a stand mixer with the paddle attachment. Add the vanilla. Mix in the flour, salt, and ginger (it's easiest to finish mixing the dough with your hands). Pat the dough into a 9-inch round cake pan. Score it into wedges with a sharp knife. Bake about 20 to 30 minutes or until the shortbread is a pale golden brown. Cool in the pan on a wire rack. While the shortbread is still warm, cut along the score lines.

Variations
Chocolate Chip: Add 1 cup chocolate chips. Omitting the ginger is optional.
Walnut: Mix 1 cup finely chopped walnuts into the dough. After the dough is in the pan, press $1/2$ cup coarsely broken walnuts into the dough. You can do the same thing with almonds, or any nuts.
Ginger Orange: Add 1 tablespoon orange zest.
Lemon: Add 1 tablespoon lemon zest.
Sea Salt: Sprinkle with several pinches of flaky sea salt. Malden and pink Hawaiian are my favorites.

Lemon Bars

Makes 24 bars

Base
$1^1/2$ cups all-purpose flour
$2/3$ cup confectioner's sugar (plus extra for dusting)
$1/4$ cup cornstarch
$3/4$ teaspoons table salt
$3/4$ cups ($1^1/2$ sticks) unsalted butter, room temperature

Filling
4 large eggs
1⅓ cups sugar
3 tablespoons all-purpose flour
⅔ cup fresh lemon juice; about 3 lemons
⅓ cup whole milk
pinch table salt

Base
Preheat oven to 350°F. Lightly grease a 9- x 13-inch pan. Combine the dry ingredients in a medium-sized bowl. Use a pastry cutter to cut the butter into the mixture until it resembles a fine meal. Press the mixture firmly into the buttered pan. Bake for 20 minutes or until the edges begin to slightly brown. Reduce oven temperature to 325°F.

Filling
Whisk all of the filling ingredients in a medium-sized bowl. Pour the filling over the warm crust and bake an additional 20 minutes or until the filling has just set. Cool completely in the pan on a wire rack and cut into bars. Dust with the confectioner's sugar.

Triple Ginger Biscotti

This recipe was given to me by guest, Robin Romero. Makes 2 dozen

$1/2$ cup (1 stick) unsalted butter (plus extra for your hands)
$3/4$ cup firmly packed dark brown sugar
2 tablespoons molasses
2 large eggs
2 tablespoons peeled and grated fresh ginger
$2/3$ cup minced crystallized ginger
$2^1/4$ cups all-purpose flour
2 teaspoons ground ginger
$1^1/2$ teaspoons baking powder
$1/4$ teaspoon table salt
3 ounces white chocolate chips; about $1/2$ cup chips

Preheat oven to 325°F. Lightly grease a baking sheet. Cream the butter and sugar with a wooden spoon or the bowl of a stand mixer with the paddle attachment. Add the molasses, eggs, and the gingers. Sift in the dry ingredients. The dough will be stiff and sticky. Butter your hands well, form the dough into 2 logs about 15 inches long, and transfer to the prepared sheet. Bake for 30 minutes. Transfer the logs from the sheet to a wire rack and cool for 5 to 10 minutes. While still warm, slice the logs at an angle with a serrated knife into $3/4$-inch slices. Place the slices on an ungreased baking sheet and bake for an additional 15 minutes. Remove from the pan and cool on a wire rack.

Melt the chocolate until smooth and transfer to a piping bag. Zig-zag the chocolate over the biscotti.

Cranberry Almond Biscotti

A guest of ours, Lauren Hubbell, gave this recipe to me. To dress them up a bit, dip one end of the biscotti into melted semisweet chocolate and place on parchment paper to cool. Biscotti are crunchy and store well. They're excellent for dipping into coffee, hot cocoa, or whatever you'd like.
Makes 2 dozen

1 cup sugar
1 teaspoon baking powder
$1/2$ teaspoon baking soda
$1/2$ teaspoon table salt

4 large eggs
1 teaspoon vanilla extract
1¼ cups dried cranberries
1 cup whole almonds
1 tablespoon unsalted butter (for your hands)

Preheat oven to 325°F. Lightly grease a baking sheet. Mix together all the ingredients. The dough will be stiff and sticky. Butter your hands well, form the dough into 2 logs about 15 inches long, and transfer to the prepared sheet. Bake for 30 minutes. Transfer the logs from the sheet to a wire rack and cool for 5 to 10 minutes. Reduce the oven temperature to 300°F. While still warm, slice the logs at an angle with a serrated knife into ¾-inch slices. Place the slices on an ungreased baking sheet and bake for an additional 20 minutes. Remove from the pan and cool on a wire rack.

Grandma's Ginger Cookies

Makes 2 dozen

$^3/_4$ cup (1$^1/_2$ sticks) unsalted butter, room temperature
1 cup firmly packed light brown sugar
1 large egg
$^1/_4$ cup molasses
$^1/_4$ teaspoon table salt
2$^1/_4$ cups all-purpose flour
2 teaspoons baking soda
$^1/_2$ teaspoon ground cloves
1 teaspoon ground cinnamon
1 teaspoon powdered ginger
sugar for rolling

Preheat the oven to 375°F. Cream the butter and sugar in a medium-sized bowl with a wooden spoon or the bowl of a stand mixer with the paddle attachment. Add the egg and molasses. Sift in the remaining ingredients. Form the dough into 1-inch balls, roll them in a small bowl of sugar, and place on an ungreased baking sheet. Space evenly apart using two baking sheets. Bake for 10 minutes or until the edges are crisp but the centers are still soft. Remove from the sheet and cool on a wire rack.

Variations
Bars: Spread the dough evenly in a greased 9- x 13-inch pan. Sprinkle with maple or demerara sugar. Bake at 350°F for about 30 to 35 minutes.
Chocolate Ginger: Add 2 cups chocolate chips and $^1/_4$ cup minced crystallized ginger.
Lemon Ginger: Add 1 teaspoon lemon extract and 2 teaspoons lemon zest.

Thick & Chewy Double Chocolate Cookies

Makes 2 dozen

16 ounces semisweet chocolate (either chips or coarsely chopped);
    about 3 cups
4 large eggs
2 teaspoons vanilla extract
2 teaspoons espresso powder or instant coffee
10 tablespoons (1 stick plus 2 tablespoons) unsalted butter,
    room temperature
1½ cups firmly packed light brown sugar
½ cup sugar
2 cups all-purpose flour
½ cup Dutch cocoa powder
2 teaspoons baking powder
1 teaspoon table salt

Preheat oven to 350°F. Melt the chocolate in a double boiler until the chocolate is almost melted. Remove from heat and stir occasionally until the chocolate is completely melted and cooled to room temperature. Meanwhile, whisk the eggs, vanilla and espresso powder in a small bowl and set aside. Cream the butter and both sugars in a large bowl with a wooden spoon or the bowl of a stand mixer with the paddle attachment. Add the egg mixture and then the chocolate until combined. Sift the flour, cocoa, baking powder, and salt into the mixture until just combined. Cover with plastic wrap and let stand at room temperature for 30 minutes or until it firms up to a fudge-like consistency. Line 2 baking sheets with parchment paper. Form 1-inch balls and place them 1½ inches apart on the baking sheet. Bake about 10 minutes. Remove the cookies from the sheets and cool on a wire rack.

Variation
Bars: Spread the dough evenly in a lightly greased 9- x 13-inch pan and bake at 350°F for about 30 to 40 minutes

Apricot Ginger Pound Cake with Rum Glaze

Serves 12 to 16

Cake
1½ cups (3 sticks) unsalted butter, room temperature
3 cups sugar
7 large eggs
1½ teaspoons vanilla extract
⅓ cup sour cream
⅓ cup whole milk
3½ cups all-purpose flour (plus extra for the pan)
¾ teaspoon table salt
½ teaspoon baking powder
¼ cup coarsely chopped crystallized ginger
½ cup coarsely chopped dried apricots

Glaze
2 tablespoons dark rum
2 tablespoons fresh orange juice
¾ cup sugar

Cake
Preheat oven to 325°F. Lightly grease and flour a bundt pan. Cream the butter and sugar in a large bowl with a wooden spoon or the bowl of a stand mixer with the paddle attachment. Add the eggs one at a time, and then vanilla, sour cream, and milk. Sift in the flour, salt, and baking powder and stir until just combined. Add the ginger and apricots. Spread the batter evenly in the prepared pan and bake until the cake springs back when lightly touched in the center, about 1 hour and 10 minutes. Cool the cake upright on a wire rack for about 10 minutes before removing.

Glaze
Whisk the glaze ingredients in a small bowl or sauce pan. Heat briefly until the sugar dissolves. Use a pastry brush to brush the surface of the warm cake with the glaze.

Variations
Maine Blueberry Ricotta and Lime: Replace ginger and apricots with 2 cups fresh or frozen Maine blueberries. Replace sour cream and milk with 1 cup whole milk ricotta. Add 2 teaspoons lime zest. For the glaze replace rum and orange juice with equal amounts fresh lime juice.

Cranberry, Almond, and Clementine: Replace ginger and apricots with 2 cups fresh or dried cranberries. Add 1½ cups chopped almonds and 2 teaspoons clementine zest. For the glaze replace rum and orange juice with equal amounts bourbon and fresh clementine juice.

Orange, Marmalade, and Chocolate: Replace ginger and apricots with 2 cups chocolate chips. For the glaze replace the sugar with ¾ cup marmalade.

Bundtlings (Mini-bundt Cakes): Reduce baking time to 15 to 20 minutes. One recipe makes 24 bundtlings.

Cake: Reduce baking time to 40 to 45 minutes. One recipe makes 2, 9-inch cake rounds.

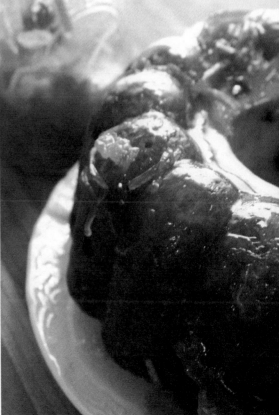

Lemon Thyme Bundt Cake

Serves 12 to 16

1½ cups (3 sticks) butter, room temperature
1¾ cup sugar (for the batter and the egg whites)
8 large eggs, separated
1 tablespoon lemon zest; about 1 lemon
2 tablespoons fresh lemon juice; about ½ lemon
1 teaspoon lemon extract
¼ cup whole milk
2¼ cups all-purpose flour (plus extra for the pan)
2 teaspoons baking powder
¼ teaspoon table salt
1 teaspoon cream of tartar
¾ cup sugar
½ cup fresh whole lemon thyme leaves (you can substitute regular fresh
    thyme if lemon-thyme is not available)

Preheat oven to 325°F. Lightly grease and flour a bundt pan. Cream the butter and
1 cup of sugar in a large bowl with a wooden spoon or the bowl of a stand mixer with
the paddle attachment and then add the egg yolks. Add the lemon zest, lemon juice,
lemon extract, and milk into the creamed butter and sugar mixture. Sift in the dry
ingredients (except the cream of tartar) into the batter and combine at low speed. In
a separate bowl, whisk the egg whites and cream of tartar until foamy. Add ¾ cup of
sugar and beat until stiff peaks form. Gently fold the egg whites and thyme leaves into
the batter. Spoon the batter into the prepared pan and bake for 1¼ to 1½ hours or
until a toothpick comes out clean and the cake springs back when lightly pressed. Cool
in the pan for 10 minutes on a wire rack before removing

Fresh Lime Pie

Serves 8

1½ cup graham cracker crumbs
4 tablespoons sugar (for both the custard and the egg whites)
5 tablespoons unsalted butter, melted
1 (14-ounce) can sweetened condensed milk
½ cup fresh lime juice; about 4 limes
2 large eggs, separated
½ teaspoon vanilla extract
4 drops green food coloring gel (optional)

whipped cream for garnish
fresh cherries for garnish
candied lime peel for garnish

Preheat oven to 325°F. Mix the graham cracker crumbs, 3 tablespoons sugar, and melted butter together in a medium bowl. Press the mixture into an 8- or 9-inch pie pan and chill for 15 minutes. Bake for 10 minutes or until the crust is firm and crisp. Meanwhile, combine the condensed milk, lime juice, egg yolks, and vanilla in a medium-sized bowl and beat until smooth and thick. In a separate bowl, whisk the whites until they hold soft peaks. Add 1 tablespoon of sugar to the whites and continue beating until stiff. Fold the whites into the lime mixture and turn into the prepared shell. Bake for 15 minutes or until the filling is set. Cool in the pan on a wire rack. Chill and serve cold.

Variation
Individual: Reduce the crust ingredients by one-third and divide between 6, 8-ounce ramekins. Follow the rest of the instructions above dividing the custard between the 6 ramekins. Note: If you use ball jars, the glass must be cooled to just warm before adding the custard.

Butterscotch-Topped Gingerbread with Sautéed Apples

Serves 12

6 tablespoons ($^3/_4$ stick) unsalted butter
$^3/_4$ cup firmly packed light brown sugar
$2^3/_4$ cups cake flour
1 teaspoon baking powder
$1^1/_2$ teaspoon baking soda
$^1/_4$ teaspoon table salt
1 tablespoon ground ginger
1 tablespoon ground cinnamon
$^1/_4$ teaspoon ground cloves
$^1/_2$ cup (1 stick) unsalted butter, room temperature
$^1/_2$ cup sugar
1 teaspoon baking soda
1 cup molasses
$1^1/_2$ cups boiling water
2 large eggs

Sautéed Apples
3 tablespoons unsalted butter
2 tablespoons sugar
4 medium apples, peeled, cored, and cut into $^1/_4$-inch wedges
whipped cream for garnish

Preheat oven to 300°F. Butter and flour the sides (not the bottom) of a 10-inch round cake pan or cast-iron skillet. Melt $^3/_4$ cup butter and brown sugar together in a small saucepan over medium heat. Pour the mixture into the cake pan and swirl it to cover the bottom..

Sift the flour, baking powder $^1/_2$ teaspoon of baking soda, salt, and spices into a medium bowl and set aside. Cream the butter and sugar in a large bowl with a wooden spoon or the bowl of a stand mixer with the paddle attachment. Meanwhile, stir 1 teaspoon of baking soda vigorously into the molasses for 1 to 2 minutes or until the molasses has lightened. Add the molasses to the creamed butter and sugar. Add the flour mixture. Add the water and combine until just smooth. Finally add the eggs one at a time, mixing thoroughly each time. The batter will be very thin. Pour the batter into the prepared pan. Bake about 1 hour and 15 minutes or until a toothpick comes out clean. Cool in the pan for 5 minutes on a wire rack. Invert the cake onto a serving plate. Serve warm with the sautéed apples.

Sautéed Apples
Cook the apples over medium heat with the butter and sugar. Allow the apples to cool slightly, then top the cake with the warm apples and serve with whipped cream.

Apple Crisp

This recipe is adapted this from the original which came from Ellen Barnes. It can be made with an endless variety of fresh fruit or combination of fruits: rhubarb, peaches, plums, raspberries, blueberries, and strawberries. For more juicy fruits, add a bit of flour to the filling as a thickener. Serves 12

Filling
4 pounds tart apples, peeled, cored, and sliced into 1/4-inch wedges;
    about 12 apples
1 cup sugar
1/2 teaspoon ground cloves
1 teaspoon ground cinnamon
1 tablespoon plus 1 teaspoon fresh lemon juice

Topping
2 1/4 cups all-purpose flour
1 1/2 cups sugar
1/4 teaspoon table salt
1 cup plus 2 tablespoons (2 1/4 sticks) unsalted butter

Filling
Preheat oven to 400°F. Combine the apples with the rest of the filling ingredients in a 9- x 13-inch pan and. Measure the flour, sugar, and salt into a medium-sized bowl. Use a pastry cutter to cut the butter into the mixture until it resembles a coarse meal.

Topping
Combine all topping ingredients in a medium-sized bowl. Sprinkle over the apple mixture and bake for 45 minutes or until the top is browned and the liquid in the apples is dark.

Chocolate Decadence Pie

One of my mess cooks dubbed this the "If-you-aren't-going-to-eat-that-then-I-will Pie". She may have had more than one piece at a sitting most times. Serves 8

$^{1}/_{2}$ cup (1 stick) unsalted butter, melted
1 (9 ounce) package chocolate wafer cookies, crushed; 40 wafers
1 (8-ounce) package cream cheese, room temperature
1 ounce (1 square) unsweetened chocolate
6 ounces semisweet chocolate chips; 1 cup chips
$^{1}/_{4}$ cup half and half
2 large eggs
$^{1}/_{2}$ teaspoon peppermint extract
$^{1}/_{2}$ cup whipping cream for garnish

Preheat oven to 350°F. Pulse the melted butter with the crushed wafers in a food processor. Press the mixture into the bottom and sides of a 10-inch pie pan. Bake the crust for 15 minutes. Meanwhile, melt the chocolate and half and half in a small sauce pan over medium heat. Whip the cream cheese in a large bowl with a wooden spoon or the bowl of a stand mixer with the whisk attachment. Gradually add the melted chocolate mixture, scraping down the sides of the bowl occasionally. Add the eggs and the extract.

Pour the chocolate mixture into the warm crust and bake for 15 to 20 minutes or until the center is just a little wiggly. Cool in the pan for at least 10 minutes on a wire rack before serving. Alternately serve room temperature or chilled. While the pie is cooling, whisk the whipping cream in a small bowl to soft peaks. Garnish the pie with a dollop of whipped cream.

Variations
Cinnamon: Replace the peppermint extract with vanilla extract. Add 1 teaspoon cinnamon.
Almond: Replace the peppermint extract with almond extract.
Orange: Replace the peppermint extract with orange extract. Garnish with candied orange peel.

Bourbon Street Bread Pudding

This is one of my favorites — and I don't even like bread pudding! Serves 9

Pudding
day-old French bread, sliced 1-inch thick, enough to cover the
   bottom of a 9-inch square pan.
$\frac{1}{2}$ cup (1 stick) unsalted butter, room temperature
1 cup sugar
5 large eggs
2 cups heavy cream
$\frac{1}{4}$ teaspoon ground cinnamon
1 tablespoon vanilla extract
$\frac{3}{4}$ cup raisins

Bourbon Sauce
1 cup sugar
1 cup heavy cream
1 tablespoon unsalted butter
dash of ground cinnamon
$\frac{1}{2}$ teaspoon cornstarch dissolved in $\frac{1}{4}$ cup water
$\frac{1}{4}$ cup bourbon

Pudding
Preheat oven to 350°F. Lightly grease a 9-inch square baking pan. Arrange the sliced
bread in one layer in the bottom of the pan. If there are large gaps, cut some pieces to
fit. Cream the butter and sugar in a medium bowl with a wooden spoon or the bowl
of a stand mixer with the paddle attachment. Add the rest of the ingredients and mix
well. Pour the mixture over the bread and let stand for at least 5 minutes. Turn the
bread over and let stand another 10 minutes. Cover the pan with foil and place it in a
larger pan filled halfway with warm tap water. Bake for 30 minutes. Remove foil and
bake for another 10 to 15 minutes. The custard should still be soft when done. Cool
slightly in the pan on a wire rack.

Bourbon Sauce
Combine all the sauce ingredients except for the bourbon in a saucepan and bring to
a boil. Continue to boil until the sauce has thickened so it coats the back of a spoon.
Remove the pan from the heat and add the bourbon. Cut the pudding into squares
and serve with the warm sauce.

Pumpkin Cheesecake

Serves 10 to 12

Cheesecake
1 cup graham cracker crumbs
1/4 cup (1/2 stick) unsalted butter, melted
1 1/2 teaspoon ground cinnamon (for both crust and filling)
2 (8-ounce) packages cream cheese
3/4 cup sugar
2 large eggs
1 cup canned pumpkin
2 tablespoons all-purpose flour
1/8 teaspoon table salt
1/2 teaspoon ground cinnamon
1/4 teaspoon ground nutmeg
1/8 teaspoon ground cloves
1/8 teaspoon ground ginger

Streusel (optional)
1/3 cup flour
1/4 cup packed brown sugar
2 tablespoons salted butter, cut into 1/4-inch cubes
1/3 cup coarsely chopped pecans
1 tablespoon minced crystallized ginger
1 teaspoon ground cinnamon
1/4 teaspoon freshly grated nutmeg

Preheat oven to 325°F. Combine the graham cracker crumbs, 1 teaspoon cinnamon, and melted butter in a small bowl. Press the mixture into the bottom of a spring form pan and bake the crust for 15 minutes. Reduce oven to 300°F. Whisk the cream cheese in a mixing bowl with the whisk attachment. Gradually add the sugar, the eggs one at a time, and the pumpkin. Sift in the dry ingredients including 1/2 teaspoon of cinnamon and mix well. Pour the batter into the prepared pan. Combine optional streusel ingredients in a small bowl and sprinkle on top. Bake for 50 minutes to 1 hour or until the middle 2 inches are still jiggly in the center. Cool in the oven with the door propped open. Chill for at least 4 hours or overnight.

Variation
Ginger Pumpkin Cheesecake: Replace graham cracker crumbs with ginger snap cookie crumbs. Add 1/4 cup minced crystallized ginger.

Pie Crust

Makes 2 crusts

2 cups all-purpose flour
1 teaspoon table salt
$^3/_4$ cup (1$^1/_2$ stick) unsalted butter, chilled and cut into $^1/_2$-inch cubes
$^1/_4$ cup ice cold water (or more)

Combine the flour, salt, and butter on the countertop by using the palm of your hands to smear the butter into the flour. In the end, it should resemble a coarse meal with a few bigger patches of butter. Transfer to a medium-sized bowl and add the water. Combine with a wooden spoon by folding in from the edges until the dough forms a workable ball. Adding more water is better than less. Form into two discs, wrap in plastic wrap, and chill for at least 30 minutes or overnight. Follow instructions for the specific recipe to either blind bake the crust or bake with the pie filling.

Black Bottom Banana Cream Pie

This is hands down, Capt. Jon's favorite pie. As you'll see, there are a number of bowls and pans required to make this recipe. It wouldn't hurt to have a dishwasher at the ready so you don't lose steam. However, it's so delicious it's worth it. Serves 8

1 pie crust (see above)

Ganache
4 ounces bittersweet chocolate, coarsely chopped
6 tablespoons whipping cream
2 tablespoons unsalted butter
2 firm, ripe bananas, peeled and cut into $^1/_2$-inch slices

Custard
1$^1/_2$ teaspoons vanilla extract
1$^1/_2$ teaspoons dark rum
1 teaspoon unflavored gelatin
1 cup whipping cream (to heat and whip)
5 large egg yolks
3 tablespoons sugar
$^1/_2$ cup whipping cream

Topping
3/4 cup whipping cream
2 tablespoons sugar
2 firm ripe bananas, peeled and cut into 1/2-inch slices

Preheat oven to 350°F. Roll out the pie crust and place it in a 9-inch pie pan. Freeze for 15 minutes then cover the bottom of the crust with dried beans (to keep it flat while it bakes) and bake about 10 to 15 minutes or until set. Cool completely on a wire rack.

Ganache
Melt the chocolate, cream, and butter in a small saucepan over medium heat. Spread the ganache into the cooled crust. Press the bananas into the ganache.

Custard
Combine vanilla and rum in a small bowl and sprinkle gelatin over the mixture. Let stand 10 minutes. Meanwhile, bring 1/2 cup whipping cream to a simmer. Whisk the egg yolks and sugar together in a separate bowl; then slowly whisk the mixture into the cream. Stir the mixture over low heat until it thickens to a ribbon-like consistency. Add the gelatin mixture and stir to completely incorporate. Transfer to another bowl and chill, stirring occasionally until cool, but not completely set. Lastly, whip the other 1/2 cup whipping cream in a small bowl. Fold the whipped cream into the custard. Spoon the mixture into the pie crust and refrigerate for 2 hours or overnight.

Topping
Whisk the cream and sugar in a small bowl. Spread the whipped cream on top of the chilled pie and arrange banana slices.

Drop Strawberry Shortcake

Serves 6 to 8

1 quart strawberries, washed and sliced
³/₄ cup sugar

Shortcake
2 cups all-purpose flour
³/₄ teaspoon table salt
1 tablespoon baking powder
3 tablespoons sugar
1 teaspoon lemon zest
¹/₂ teaspoon ground nutmeg
¹/₄ cup (¹/₂ stick) unsalted butter, chilled and cut into ¹/₂-inch cubes
1 cup buttermilk

Whipped Cream
1 cup heavy cream
3 tablespoons sugar
¹/₂ teaspoons vanilla extract

Preheat oven to 350°F. Mix the sliced strawberries and sugar together in a large bowl and set aside for at least one hour (to allow the juice to develop). Sift the dry ingredients into a large bowl. Use a pastry cutter to cut the butter into the mixture until it resembles a coarse meal. Stir in the buttermilk until the mixture is just blended. Spoon 6 to 8 biscuits onto an ungreased baking pan and bake for 12 minutes or until lightly browned.

When the biscuits are done, whip the cream, sugar, and vanilla in a medium-sized bowl. To serve, cut the shortcakes in half, spoon the berries on top of the bottom half of the shortcake, place the top half of the shortcake on the berries, and garnish with whipped cream.

Variation
Rhubarb: Heat 8 cups diced rhubarb, 1¹/₂ cups sugar, and ¹/₂ teaspoon cinnamon in a saucepan until the rhubarb has softened and broken apart some. Serve warm or chilled.

Mom's Pecan Pie

Serves 8

1 unbaked pie crust (page 192)
4 large eggs
1 cup sugar
3 tablespoons all-purpose flour
1 cup dark corn syrup
½ teaspoon table salt
3 tablespoons unsalted butter, melted
2 teaspoons vanilla extract
1 cup whole pecans
pinch table salt

Preheat oven to 350°F. Dust the counter with a little flour and roll the pie crust into
an 11-inch round. Transfer to a 9-inch pie pan and pinch the edges. Whisk the eggs
together in a medium bowl. Add the sugar, flour, syrup, salt, butter, and extract. Stir in
the pecans. Pour the filling into the unbaked pie shell and bake for 35 to 40 minutes or
until the nuts are golden brown and the center jiggles just a tiny bit.

Ginger Ice Cream

This recipe is in honor of a crew member who was with us for several years. He turned me on to ginger beer, although the one he likes will blow the back of your head off. He had a penchant for sneaking down into the galley and adding a pinch or more of ginger to whatever I was making. THIS recipe has enough ginger in it! Makes 1 quart

¹⁄₂ cup sugar
¹⁄₄ cup grated fresh ginger
2 tablespoons water
2 cups half and half
4 large egg yolks
1 cup heavy cream
1 teaspoon vanilla extract
¹⁄₂ cup minced crystallized ginger

In a medium saucepan, heat the sugar, fresh ginger, and water over medium-high heat, stirring occasionally, for 5 minutes or until the sugar has melted. Stir in the half and half and bring to a simmer, stirring often. In a separate bowl, whisk the egg yolks and gradually add the half and half mixture in a slow stream, whisking constantly. Pour the mixture back into the saucepan and cook over medium-low heat, stirring constantly, until a thermometer registers 170°F (do not let boil). Pour the custard through a sieve into a clean bowl and stir in the heavy cream and vanilla. Cover the surface of the mixture with plastic wrap and chill until cold. Follow the instructions for your electric or hand-cranked ice cream maker. Once the ice cream has stiffened, add the crystallized ginger and mix for another 2 minutes.

Super Fresh Berry Pie

Serves 8

1 pie crust (page 192)
4 cups fresh Maine blueberries or mixed berries
1 cup sugar (plus 2 tablespoons the whipped cream)
2 tablespoons cornstarch (3 if the berries are really juicy)
pinch table salt
2 cups heavy cream
1 teaspoon vanilla extract

Preheat oven to 350°F. Roll out the pie crust and place it in a 9-inch pie pan. Freeze for 15 minutes then cover the bottom of the crust with dried beans (to keep it flat while it bakes) and bake for 10 to 15 minutes or until set. Cool completely on a wire rack.

Place 2 cups of berries in the baked pie shell. Mash 2 cups of berries in a saucepan with 1 cup sugar, the cornstarch, and salt. Bring the mixture to a boil over medium-high heat until the liquid is thick and clear. Pour the hot berries over the berries in the pie shell and spread evenly. Refrigerate for at least 1 hour or overnight. Just before serving, whip the cream, 2 tablespoons sugar, and vanilla to stiff peaks in a large bowl by hand or in a mixing bowl with the whisk attachment. Spread on top of the chilled berry pie and serve.

Variation
Almond Berry Pie: Replace almond extract with vanilla extract.

Mom's Chocolate Cake

Serves 10 to 12

Cake
½ cup (1 stick) unsalted butter, room temperature
1 cup sugar
1 large egg
3 ounces (3 squares) unsweetened chocolate, melted
1 teaspoon vanilla extract
1⅓ cups all-purpose flour
1 teaspoon baking powder
1 teaspoon baking soda
½ teaspoon table salt
1 cup freshly brewed coffee

Frosting
¼ cup (½ stick) unsalted butter, room temperature
1½ cups confectioner's sugar
1 teaspoon vanilla extract
2 tablespoons whole milk
4 ounces (4 squares) unsweetened chocolate, melted

Cake
Preheat oven to 350°F. Lightly grease an 8- or 9-inch round cake pan. Cream the butter and sugar in a large bowl with a wooden spoon or the bowl of a stand mixer with the paddle attachment and then add the egg. Stir in the melted chocolate and vanilla. Sift in the dry ingredients alternating with the coffee until fully incorporated. Pour the batter into the prepared pan and bake for 20 to 25 minutes or until a toothpick inserted comes out clean and the cake springs back when lightly pressed. Cool in the pan for 10 minutes on a wire rack before removing to cool completely.

Frosting
While the cake cools, cream the butter in a mixing bowl with the whisk attachment. Add the rest of the ingredients and whisk until smooth and the frosting is spreadable.

Variations
Super Rich Chocolate Cake: Replace ⅓ cup flour with ⅓ cup black cocoa powder.
Chocolate Whiskey Cake: Replace ½ cup coffee with ½ cup good whiskey. Omit the chocolate from the frosting. Add extra confectioner's sugar and replace the milk with whiskey.

Happenings and Lore

These little stories are part lore, part community, and part context for the *Riggin*. They are a collection of snippets, traditions, history, and happenings. How we operate the boat as a business and as an extension of our community can be chronicled by little moments such as these.

Low Rider

Our nickname in the fleet is "Low Rider" because our hull is sleek and low to the water. During the summer we will often anchor together for festivals and raftups (when all the boats tie up side by side); occasionally the crews of each boat play pranks on each other. The morning after one such raftup, we found this nickname written as a license plate on our transom. There was a pair of "fuzzy dice" hanging off the bowsprit as well.

A Little TLC

When we bought our house, the realtor said it needed a little TLC. This is realtor speak for "You'll need to gut the place." Our gardens and lawn were in the same shape — a few shoes and engine parts sticking up between patches of grass, but no flowers or herbs unless you count the comfrey taking charge in the back yard. It's been an ongoing project, but gradually, each year, I add more tilled area so that now we have over 3,000 square feet of garden from which I bring all of the herbs and flowers we use on the boat. Growing my own herbs means using them with an abandon I never would if I actually paid for them at the grocery store.

One Ringie-Dingie

The ringing of bells on board ships has been a tradition from the earliest days of sail. Bells are used for signaling, keeping time, raising an alarm, and more recently, calling everyone to meals. The ringing of the ship's bell for meals is a ritual we keep on the *J. & E. Riggin*. The system is based on the four-hour watch typical on naval vessels. The watches run from 8 a.m. to 12 noon, 12 noon to 4 p.m., 4 p.m. to 8 p.m., and so on. A bell is struck once at the end of the first half hour of a four-hour watch, twice after the first hour, etc. until eight bells mark the end of the watch. We eat at 8 a.m., 12 noon, and 6 p.m. and therefore ring 8 bells, 8 bells, and 4 bells respectively. Guests often tell us that after returning home, the sound of a bell causes them to automatically think it's time to eat! Pavlov was on to something.

Charlie Who?

Charlie Noble is an "it", not a "he". It's the nickname for the galley smokestack. A British merchant service captain, Charles Noble, is said to be responsible for the origin of the name around 1850. It seems that upon discovering that the stack of his ship's galley was made of copper, Captain Noble ordered that it be kept brightly polished. The ship's crew then stared referring to the stack as "Charlie Noble".

"Because Dottie yelled at me"

I'd been planning to write the first edition of this cookbook from the beginning, but toddlers and boat projects took priority for a number of winters. Instead, after each sailing trip, I would find myself dictating recipes while guests eagerly wrote them down. Each week I promised there would be a cookbook "someday". One summer, I got a slightly firmer nudge to get serious about the cookbook. A lovely, mild-mannered repeat guest of ours, one who comes at least once a year with her husband and who works in marketing, took me firmly by the shoulders, leaned forward (basically in my face) and shouted, "If you made a cookbook, people would buy it!" She was right. Since then, I've been saying that I wrote the cookbook because Dottie yelled at me.

Acknowledgments

The idea for this cookbook began almost from the day we bought the Schooner *J. & E. Riggin*, however, dreaming and doing are two very different things. I knew that when the time was right, the perfect partners would present themselves— and I wasn't wrong. Frank Chillemi, a guest who just happens to be an award-winning photographer, led the photography for the first edition. His photos are now complimented by Elizabeth Poisson's work in this second edition. Dana Dagenhardt, a project manager specializing in books and software packages, became the project manager for the first edition. She also is a Culinary Institute of Art graduate and loves to do all of the things I'm not good at— edit, design, futz, details, details, details. For the second edition, Elizabeth Poisson stepped in to manage the project. Her attention to detail rivals any, Dana included! My work is made better by these individuals through their talent, collaboration, and generous spirits. I am deeply grateful to them all.

In addition to creating a second edition of the cookbook, we ran a Kickstarter campaign which allowed pre-orders of the book to fund the printing costs. It was a fabulous success! We could not have done it without our one hundred twenty-three backers. A special thanks to those who were able to be super generous. In no particular order, but with a massive dollop of appreciation: Louisa Enright, Kate Watson, Bernard Allanson, Jill van den Heuvel, Katherine Sproull, Alleson Bixler, Andy Seestedt, and Norma Hunt Mahle.

Throughout my cooking and sailing life, two people have been my mentors. Ellen Barnes, my boss on the first windjammer I ever worked on, taught me to not just talk but to do. She and her husband, Ken Barnes, have watched me become a grown-up, a wife, a business owner, and a parent. Her advice has been refreshing, honest, and invaluable. Hans Bucher, Chef/Owner at Jessica's Restaurant taught me how to make food taste good all the time. The rare camaraderie we shared working side-by-side in a small, hot kitchen will always be treasured.

To Kara Plikaitis for her creativity, inspiration, and visual clarity. And to MORE and Co. for their initial design and concept work. To Norma Mahle, Jesse Ellis, and Ella Finger, for your sharp eyes and your willingness to look at anything I sent you.

To ALL of the recipe testers whether on the *Riggin*, in my home, or in your own homes; your feedback is invaluable. This is my team in no particular order: Patricia Johns, Diane Agostino, Jane Peak, Ann Pare, Pinky Rines, Cindy Frederick, Susan Land, Julie Thiessen, Patricia Wisneski, Tish Gallagher, Karen Courington, Amy

Wilke, Susy Ellis, Beth Long, Lisa Nicklow, Nancy West, Kelly Evenson, Lynn Yonally, Ellie Roberts, Andree Anne Cote, Richard Davies, Joyce Riddle, Rose Chillemi, Angie Muhs, Susan Kottel, Karen Connor, Betsy Maislen, Cindy Holden, and Christine Bond.

Thanks also to all of my mess cooks over the years that have supported this work. Your laughter, joy, eagerness, and hard work have made my work in the galley a gift. To all of the farmers, growers, and producers who have a place at my table whether through their food or their actual presence. What I create every day would pale without your attention to detail and your care of the products you grow, raise, and create.

Finally, to our guests on the *Riggin*, without their insistence, I would have never put fingertips to keyboard. Again.

Index

Index